MYTHS OF ANCIENT GREECE

ROBERT GRAVES

myths of ancient greece

ILLUSTRATED BY JOAN KIDDELL-MONROE

CASSELL · LONDON

CASSELL & COMPANY LTD
35 Red Lion Square · London wci
and at
MELBOURNE · SYDNEY · TORONTO · JOHANNESBURG
AUCKLAND

———

SBN 304 92491 1

Printed in Great Britain by
Lowe & Brydone (Printers) Ltd., London
468

INTRODUCTION

Almost all arts and useful sciences were given us by the ancient Greeks: such as astronomy, mathematics, engineering, architecture, medicine, money, literature, and law. Even modern scientific language is mostly formed from Greek words. They were the first people in Europe to write books, and two long poems by Homer—about the siege of Troy and the adventures of Odysseus—are still read with pleasure though he lived more than seven hundred years before the birth of Christ. After Homer came Hesiod, who wrote among other things about gods, and fighting men, and the Creation. The Greeks greatly respected Homer and Hesiod, and the stories (now called "myths") which they and other poets told, became part of school education not only in Greece, but wherever the Greek language had spread—from Western Asia to North Africa and Spain.

Rome conquered Greece about one hundred and fifty years before the birth of Christ, but the Romans admired Greek poetry so much that they went on reading it even after becoming Christians. Roman school education spread all over Europe and, in the end, was brought without much change from England to America. Every educated person had to know the Greek myths almost as well as he knew the Bible, if only because the Greek map of the night-sky, still used by astronomers, was a picture book of myths. Groups of stars made outlines of people and animals mentioned in them: heroes such as Heracles and Perseus, the Winged Horse Pegasus, beautiful Andromeda, the Serpent who nearly ate her, Orion the Hunter, Cheiron the Centaur, the stern of the *Argo*, the Ram of the Golden Fleece, and so on.

These myths are not solemn, like Bible stories. The notion that there could be only one God and no goddesses did not please the Greeks, who were a gifted, quarrelsome, humorous race. They thought of Heaven as ruled by a divine family rather like any rich human family on earth, but immortal and all-powerful; and used to poke fun at them at the same time as offering them sacrifices. In remote European villages even today, where a rich man owns most of the land and houses, much the same thing happens. Every villager is polite to the landlord and pays rent regularly. But behind his back he will often say: 'What a proud, violent, hasty-tempered fellow! How he ill-treats his wife, and how she nags at him! As for their children: they are a bad bunch! That pretty daughter is crazy about men and doesn't care how she behaves; that son in the Army is a bully and a coward; and the one who acts as his father's agent and looks after the cattle is far too smooth-tongued to be trusted... Why, the other day I heard a story . . .'

That was just how the Greeks spoke of their god Zeus, his wife Hera, his son Ares the War-god, his daughter Aphrodite, his other son Hermes, and the rest of the quarrelsome family. The Romans knew them by different names: 'Jupiter' instead of Zeus; 'Mars' instead of Ares; 'Venus' instead of Aphrodite; 'Mercury' instead of Hermes—which are now the names of planets. The fighting men, most of whom claimed to be sons of gods by human mothers, were ancient Greek kings whose adventures the poets repeated to please their proud descendants.

R.G.

Deyá,
Majorca,
Spain.

CONTENTS

MYTHS OF ANCIENT GREECE

THE PALACE OF OLYMPUS

CHAPTER ONE

*

THE PALACE OF OLYMPUS

The twelve most important gods and goddesses of ancient Greece, called the Olympians, belonged to the same large, quarrelsome family. Though thinking little of the smaller, old-fashioned gods over whom they ruled, they thought even less of mortals. All the Olympians lived together in an enormous palace, set well above the usual level of clouds at the top of Mount Olympus, the highest mountain in Greece. Great walls, too steep for climbing, protected the Palace. The Olympians' masons, gigantic one-eyed Cyclopes, had built them on much the same plan as royal palaces on earth.

At the southern end, just behind the Council Hall, and looking towards the famous Greek cities of Athens, Thebes, Sparta, Corinth, Argos, and Mycenae, were the private apartments of King Zeus, the Father-god, and Queen Hera, the Mother-goddess. The northern end of the palace, looking across the valley of Tempe towards the wild hills of Macedonia, consisted of the kitchen, banqueting hall, armoury, workshops, and servants' quarters. In between came a square court, open to the sky, with covered cloisters and private rooms on each side, belonging to the other five Olympian gods and the other five Olympian goddesses. Beyond the kitchen and servants' quarters stood cottages for smaller gods, sheds for chariots, stables for horses, kennels for hounds, and a sort of zoo where the Olympians kept their

13

sacred animals. These included a bear, a lion, a peacock, an eagle, tigers, stags, a cow, a crane, snakes, a wild boar, white bulls, a wild cat, mice, swans, herons, an owl, a tortoise, and a tank full of fish.

In the Council Hall the Olympians met at times to discuss mortal affairs—such as which army on earth should be allowed to win a war, and whether they ought to punish some king or queen who had been behaving proudly or disgustingly. But for the most part they were too busy with their own quarrels and lawsuits to take much notice of mortal affairs. King Zeus had an enormous throne of polished black Egyptian marble, decorated in gold. Seven steps led up to it, each of them enamelled with one of the seven colours of the rainbow. A bright blue covering above showed that the whole sky belonged to Zeus alone; and on the right arm of his throne perched a ruby-eyed golden eagle clutching jagged strips of pure tin, which meant that Zeus could kill whatever enemies he pleased by throwing a thunderbolt of forked lightning at them. A purple ram's fleece covered the cold seat. Zeus used it for magical rain-making in times of drought. He was a strong, brave, stupid, noisy, violent, conceited god, and always on the watch lest his family should try to get rid of him; having once himself got rid of his wicked, idle, cannibalistic father Cronus, King of the Titans and Titanesses. The Olympians could not die, but Zeus, with the help of his two elder brothers, Hades and Poseidon, had banished Cronus to a distant island in the Atlantic—perhaps the Azores, perhaps Torrey Island, off the coast of Ireland. Zeus, Hades, and Poseidon then drew lots for the three parts of Cronus's kingdom. Zeus won the sky; Poseidon, the sea; Hades, the Underworld; they shared the earth between them. One of Zeus's emblems was the eagle, another was the woodpecker.

Cronus managed at last to escape from the island in a small boat and, changing his name to Saturn, settled quietly among the Italians, and behaved very well. In fact, until Zeus discovered his escape and banished him again, Saturn's reign was known as the Golden Age. Mortals in Italy lived without work or trouble, eating only acorns, wild fruit, honey, and pig-nuts, and drinking only milk or water. They never fought wars, and spent their days dancing and singing.

Queen Hera had an ivory throne, with three crystal steps leading up to it. Golden cuckoos and willow leaves decorated the back, and a full moon hung above it. Hera sat on a white cowskin, which she sometimes used for rain-making magic if Zeus could not be bothered to stop a drought. She disliked being Zeus's wife, because he was frequently marrying mortal women and saying, with a sneer, that these marriages did not count—his brides would soon grow ugly and die; but she was his Queen, and perpetually young and beautiful.

When first asked to marry him, Hera had refused; and had gone on refusing every year for three hundred years. But one springtime Zeus disguised himself as a poor cuckoo caught in a thunderstorm, and tapped at her window. Hera, not seeing through his disguise, let the cuckoo in, stroked his wet feathers, and whispered: 'Poor bird, I love you.' At once, Zeus changed back again into his true shape, and said: 'Now you must marry me!' After this, however badly Zeus behaved, Hera felt obliged to set a good example to gods and goddesses and mortals, as the Mother of Heaven. Her emblem was the cow, the most motherly of animals; but, not wishing to be thought as plain-looking and placid as a cow, she also used the peacock and the lion.

These two thrones faced down the Council Hall towards the door leading into the open courtyard. Along the sides of the hall stood ten other thrones—for five goddesses on

Hera's side, for five gods on Zeus's.

Poseidon, god of the seas and rivers, had the second-largest throne. It was of grey-green white-streaked marble, ornamented with coral, gold, and mother-of-pearl. The arms were carved in the shape of sea-beasts, and Poseidon sat on sealskin. For his help in banishing Cronus and the Titans, Zeus had married him to Amphitrite, the former Sea-goddess, and allowed him to take over all her titles. Though Poseidon hated to be less important than his younger brother, and always went about scowling, he feared Zeus's thunderbolt. His only weapon was a trident, with which he could stir up the sea and so wreck ships; but Zeus never travelled by ship. When Poseidon felt even crosser than usual, he would drive away in his chariot to a palace under the waves, near the island of Euboea, and there let his rage cool. As his emblem Poseidon chose the horse, an animal which he pretended to have created. Large waves are still called 'white horses' because of this.

Opposite Poseidon sat his sister Demeter, goddess of all useful fruits, grasses, and grains. Her throne of bright green malachite was ornamented with ears of barley in gold, and little golden pigs for luck. Demeter seldom smiled, except when her daughter Persephone—unhappily married to the hateful Hades, God of the Dead—came to visit her once a year. Demeter had been rather wild as a girl, and nobody could remember the name of Persephone's father: probably some country god married for a drunken joke at a harvest festival. Demeter's emblem was the poppy, which grows red as blood among the barley.

Next to Poseidon sat Hephaestus, a son of Zeus and Hera. Being the god of goldsmiths, jewellers, blacksmiths, masons, and carpenters, he had built all these thrones himself, and made his own a masterpiece of every different metal and precious stone to be found. The seat could swivel about, the arms could move up and down, and the whole throne rolled along automatically wherever he wished, like the three-legged golden tables in his workshop. Hephaestus had hobbled ever since birth, when Zeus roared at Hera: 'A brat as weak as this is unworthy of me!'—and threw him far out over the walls of Olympus. In his fall Hephaestus broke a leg so badly that he had to wear a golden leg-iron. He kept a country house on Lemnos, the island where he had struck earth; and his emblem was the quail, a bird that does a hobbling dance in springtime.

Opposite Hephaestus sat Athene, Goddess of Wisdom, who first taught him how to handle tools, and knew more than anyone else about pottery, weaving, and all useful arts. Her silver throne had golden basketwork at the back and sides, and a crown of violets, made from blue lapis lazuli, set above it. Its arms ended in grinning Gorgons' heads. Athene, wise though she was, did not know the names of her parents. Poseidon claimed her as his daughter by a marriage with an African goddess called Libya. It is true that, as a child, she had been found wandering in a goatskin by the shores of a Libyan lake; but rather than admit herself the daughter of Poseidon, whom she thought very stupid, she allowed Zeus to pretend she was his. Zeus announced that one day, overcome by a fearful headache, he had howled aloud like a thousand wolves hunting in a pack. Hephaestus, he said, then ran up with an axe and kindly split open his skull, and out sprang Athene, dressed in full armour. Athene was also a Battle-goddess, yet never went to war unless forced—being too sensible to pick quarrels—and when she fought, always won. She chose the wise owl as her emblem; and had a town house at Athens.

Next to Athene sat Aphrodite, Goddess of Love and

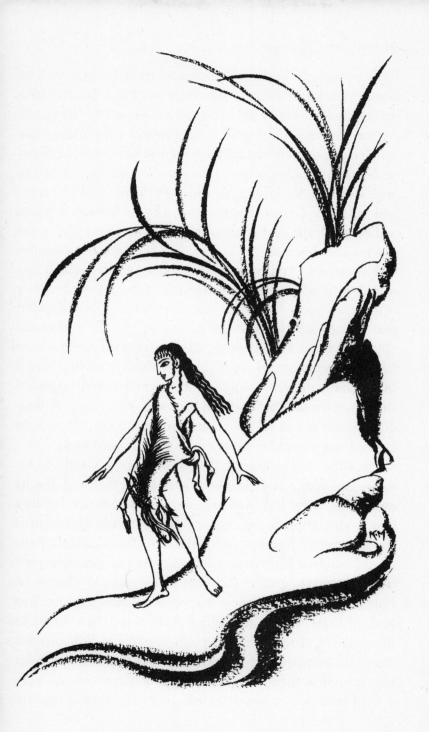

Beauty. Nobody knew who her parents were, either. The South Wind said that he had once seen her floating in a scallop shell off the island of Cythera, and steered her gently ashore. She may have been a daughter of Amphitrite by a smaller god named Triton, who used to blow roaring blasts on a conch, or perhaps by old Cronus. Amphitrite refused to say a word on the subject. Aphrodite's throne was silver, inlaid with beryls and aquamarines, the back shaped like a scallop shell, the seat made of swan's down, and under her feet lay a golden mat—an embroidery of golden bees, apples, and sparrows. Aphrodite had a magic girdle, which she would wear whenever she wanted to make anyone love her madly. To keep Aphrodite out of mischief, Zeus decided that she needed a hard-working, decent husband; and naturally chose his son Hephaestus. Hephaestus exclaimed: 'Now I am the happiest god alive!' But she thought it disgraceful to be the wife of a sooty-faced, horny-handed, crippled smith and insisted on having a bedroom of her own. Aphrodite's emblem was the dove, and she would visit Paphos, in Cyprus, once a year to swim in the sea, for good luck.

Opposite Aphrodite sat Ares, Hephaestus's tall, handsome, boastful, cruel brother, who loved fighting for its own sake. Ares and Aphrodite were continually holding hands and giggling in corners, which made Hephaestus jealous. Yet if he ever complained to the Council, Zeus would laugh at him, saying: 'Fool, why did you give your wife that magic girdle? Can you blame your brother if he falls in love with her when she wears it?' Ares's throne was built of brass, strong and ugly—those huge brass knobs in the shape of skulls, and that cushion-cover of human skin! Ares had no manners, no learning, and the worst of taste; yet Aphrodite thought him wonderful. His emblems were a wild boar and a bloodstained spear. He kept a country house among the rough woods of Thrace.

Next to Ares sat Apollo, the god of music, poetry, medicine, archery, and young unmarried men—Zeus's son by Leto, one of the smaller goddesses, whom he married to annoy Hera. Apollo rebelled against his father once or twice, but got well punished each time, and learned to behave more sensibly. His highly polished golden throne had magical inscriptions carved all over it, a back shaped like a lyre, and a python skin to sit on. Above hung a golden sun-disk with twenty-one rays shaped like arrows, because he pretended to manage the Sun. Apollo's emblem was a mouse; mice were supposed to know the secrets of earth, and tell them to him. (He preferred white mice to ordinary ones; most boys still do.) Apollo owned a splendid house at Delphi on the top of Mount Parnassus, built around the famous oracle which he stole from Mother Earth, Zeus's grandmother.

Opposite Apollo sat his twin-sister Atemis, goddess of hunting and of unmarried girls, from whom he had learned medicine and archery. Her throne was of pure silver, with a wolfskin to sit on, and the back shaped like two date palms, one on each side of a new-moon boat. Apollo married several mortal wives at different times. Once he chased a girl named Daphne, who cried out for help to Mother Earth and got turned into a laurel tree before he could catch and kiss her. Artemis, however, hated the idea of marriage, although she kindly took care of mothers when their babies were born. She much preferred hunting, fishing, and swimming in moonlit mountain pools. If any mortal happened to see her without clothes, she used to change him into a stag and hunt him to death. She chose as her emblem the she-bear, the most dangerous of all wild animals in Greece.

Last in the row of gods sat Hermes, Zeus's son by a smaller

goddess named Maia, after whom the month of May is called: Hermes, the god of merchants, bankers, thieves, fortune-tellers, and heralds, born in Arcadia. His throne was cut out of a single piece of solid grey rock, the arms shaped like rams' heads, and a goatskin for the seat. On its back he had carved a swastika, this being the shape of a fire-making machine invented by him—the fire-drill. Until then, house-wives used to borrow glowing pieces of charcoal from their neighbours. Hermes also invented the alphabet; and one of his emblems was the crane, because cranes fly in a V—the first letter he wrote. Another of Hermes's emblems was a peeled hazel stick, which he carried as the Messenger of the Olympians: white ribbons dangled from it, which foolish people often mistook for snakes.

Last in the row of goddesses sat Zeus's eldest sister, Hestia, Goddess of the Home: on a plain, uncarved, wooden throne, and a plain cushion woven of undyed wool. Hestia, the kind-est and most peaceable of all the Olympians, hated the con-tinual family quarrels, and never troubled to choose any particular emblem of her own. She used to tend the charcoal hearth in the middle of the Council Hall.

That made six gods and six goddesses. But one day Zeus announced that Dionysus, his son by a mortal woman named Semele, had invented wine, and must be given a seat in the Council. Thirteen Olympians would have been an unlucky number; so Hestia offered him her seat, just to keep the peace. Now there were seven gods and five goddesses; an unjust state of affairs because, when questions about women had to be discussed, the gods outvoted the goddesses. Diony-sus's throne was gold-plated fir wood, ornamented with bunches of grapes carved in amethyst (a violet-coloured stone), snakes carved in serpentine (a stone with many markings), and various horned animals besides, carved in onyx (a black and white stone), sard (a dark red stone), jade (a dark green stone), and carnelian (a pink stone). He took the tiger for his emblem, having once visited India at the head of a drunken army and brought tigers back as souvenirs.

Of the other gods and goddesses living on Olympus, Heracles the Porter slept in the gatehouse; and Poseidon's wife Amphitrite has already been mentioned. There were also Dionysus's mother Semele, whom he persuaded Zeus to turn into a goddess; Ares's hateful sister Eris, Goddess of Quarrels; Iris, Hera's messenger, who used to run along the rainbow; the Goddess Nemesis, who kept a list for the Olympians of proud mortals due to be punished; Aphrodite's wicked little son Eros, God of Love, who enjoyed shooting arrows at people to make them fall ridiculously in love; Hebe, Goddess of Youth, who married Heracles; Ganymede, Zeus's handsome young cup-bearer; the Nine Muses, who sang in the Banqueting Hall; and Zeus's ancient mother, Rhea, whom he treated very shabbily, though she had once saved his life by a trick when Cronus wanted to eat him.

In a room behind the kitchen sat the Three Fates, named Clotho, Lachesis, and Atropos. They were the oldest goddesses in existence, too old for anybody to remember where they came from. The Fates decided how long each mortal should live: spinning a linen thread, to measure exactly so many inches and feet for months and years, and then snipping it off with a pair of shears. They also knew, but seldom revealed, what would be the fate of each Olympian god. Even Zeus feared them for that reason.

The Olympians drank nectar, a sweet drink made from fermented honey; and ate ambrosia, said to be an uncooked mixture of honey, water, fruit, olive oil, cheese, and barley —though this may be doubted. Some claim that certain

23

speckled mushrooms were the true food of the Olympians, created whenever Zeus's thunderbolt struck the earth; and that this kept them immortal. Because the Olympians also loved the smell, though not the taste, of roast beef and mutton, mortals used to sacrifice sheep and cattle to them, afterwards eating the meat themselves.

OTHER GODS AND GODDESSES

CHAPTER TWO

*

OTHER GODS AND GODDESSES

Besides mortals on earth in those ancient days, there were a number of strong, ox-horned River-gods, each called after his particular river; and dozens of lovely immortal Naiads in charge of fountains and springs, whose permission mortals always asked before drinking—or else it would be the worse for them. These River-gods and Naiads paid homage to Poseidon; and so did the mermaids, the salt-water Nereids. But the Hamadryads in charge of oaks, and the Meliads in charge of ash trees, and the variously named other Nymphs in charge of pines, apple trees, and myrtles, all came under the rule of the Country-god Pan. If anyone tried to cut down one of these trees without first making a sacrifice to the nymph in charge—usually the sacrifice was a pig—his axe bounced off the trunk and cut his own legs.

The Great God Pan, a simple fellow, kept out of the Olympians' way, but used to protect shepherds, help hunters to find game, and go dancing in the moonlight with the nymphs. Pan was so ugly at birth that his mother, one of these nymphs, ran away from him in terror—he had little horns, a little beard, the legs, hooves, and tail of a goat. Hermes, his father, took him up to Olympus for Zeus and the other gods to laugh at. Pan loved to sleep every afternoon in a cave or forest grove and, if a passing stranger woke him by mistake, let out such a horrible yell that the stranger's hair bristled, like a hedgehog, in what is still called 'Panic' fear.

Pan once fell in love with a nymph called Pitys. She was so scared when he tried to kiss her that she turned herself into a pine tree to escape him. Pan broke off one of the pine branches, and wore it as a wreath in memory of her. Much the same thing happened when he fell in love with the nymph Syrinx: she escaped from him by changing into a reed. Unable to tell which she was among all the thousands of other reeds growing beside the river, he took a stick and angrily hit at them. Then, feeling ashamed of himself, he collected the broken reeds, cut them in different lengths with a flint knife, bored holes in their sides, and tied them in a neat row—to form a new musical instrument, called the Pan Pipe.

On an April evening, in the year A.D. 1, a ship was sailing to Northern Italy along the coast of Greece, when the crew heard distant sounds of mourning, and a loud voice from the shore shouted to one of them: 'As soon as you reach the next port, be sure to spread the sad news that the Great God Pan is dead!' But how and why he had died nobody ever knew. It may, of course, have been just a rumour put about by Apollo, who wanted Pan's temples for himself.

DEMETER'S LOST DAUGHTER

CHAPTER THREE

*

DEMETER'S LOST DAUGHTER

Hades, the gloomy God of Death, was forbidden to visit Olympus, but lived in a dark palace deep under the earth. He met his brother Zeus one day in Greece, their common ground, and confessed: 'I have fallen in love with your niece Persephone, Demeter's daughter. May I have your permission to marry her?'

Zeus feared to offend Hades by saying: 'No! What a horrible idea!' He also feared to offend Demeter by saying: 'Why not?' So, giving Hades neither a *yes* nor a *no*, he winked at him instead.

The wink satisfied Hades. He went to Colonus near Athens, where Persephone, busily picking spring flowers, had strayed away from her friends, and carried her off in his great hearse of a chariot. Persephone screamed, but when the girls came running up she was gone, leaving no trace behind her except some crushed daisies and corn-flowers. The girls told Demeter as much as they knew.

Demeter, very worried, disguised herself as an old woman and wandered through Greece searching for Persephone. Nine days she travelled, without food or drink, and nobody could give her any news. At last she headed back towards Athens. At nearby Eleusis the King and Queen treated her so kindly, offering her a position as nurse to the younger princes, that she accepted a drink of barley-water.

Presently the eldest prince, Triptolemus, who looked after the royal cows, came hurrying in. 'If I am not mistaken, my lady,' he said, 'you are the Goddess Demeter. I fear that I bring bad news. My brother Eubuleus was feeding the pigs at Colonus, not far from here, when he heard the thunder of hooves and saw a chariot rush past. In it were a dark-faced king wearing black armour, and a frightened girl who looked like your daughter Persephone. Then the earth opened before my brother's eyes, and down the chariot rushed. All our pigs fell in after it and were lost; for the earth closed over the hole again.'

Demeter guessed that the dark-faced king must have been Hades. With her friend, the old Witch-goddess Hecate, she questioned the Sun, who sees all. The Sun refused to answer, but Hecate threatened to eclipse him every day at noon if he would not tell them the truth. 'It *was* King Hades,' the Sun confessed.

'My brother Zeus must have plotted this!' said Demeter in a fury. 'I will be revenged on him.'

She would not return to Olympus, but wandered about Greece, forbidding her trees to bear fruit, or her grass to grow for the cattle to eat. If this went on much longer, mankind would surely die of hunger; so Zeus made Hera send her messenger Iris down the rainbow with a message to Demeter: 'Please be sensible, dear Sister, and let things grow again!' When Demeter took no notice, Zeus sent Poseidon, and Hestia, and Hera herself, to offer her wonderful presents. But Demeter groaned: 'Take them away. I shall do nothing for any of you, ever, until my daughter comes home to me!'

Then Zeus sent Hermes to tell Hades: 'Unless you let that girl go home, Brother, we shall all be ruined.' He also gave Hermes a message for Demeter: 'You may have Persephone back, so long as she has not yet tasted the Food of the Dead.'

Since Persephone had refused to eat even a crust of bread, saying that she would rather starve, Hades could hardly pretend that she had gone off with him willingly. Deciding to obey Zeus, he called Persephone and said kindly: 'You seem unhappy here, my dear. You have taken no nourishment at all. Perhaps you had better go home.'

One of Hades's gardeners, called Ascalaphus, began to hoot with laughter. 'Taken no nourishment at all, you say? This very morning I saw her pick a pomegranate from your underground orchard.'

Hades smiled to himself. He brought Persephone in his chariot to Eleusis, where Demeter hugged her and cried for pleasure. Hades then said: 'By the way, Persephone ate seven red pomegranate seeds—this gardener of mine saw her. She must come down to Tartarus again.'

'If she goes,' screamed Demeter, 'I shall never lift my curse from the earth, but let all men and animals die!'

In the end, Zeus sent Rhea (who was Demeter's mother as well as his own) to plead with her. The two at last agreed that Persephone should marry Hades, and spend seven months of the year in Tartarus, one month for each pomegranate seed eaten, and the rest above ground.

Demeter punished Ascalaphus by turning him into a hooting long-eared owl; but she rewarded Triptolemus by giving him a bag of barley seed and a plough. At her orders, he went all over the world in a chariot drawn by snakes, teaching mankind how to plough the fields, sow barley seed, and reap the harvest.

THE TITANS

CHAPTER FOUR

*

THE TITANS

The Titans and Titanesses, led by King Cronus, had ruled the world until Zeus's rebellion put the Olympians in power. There were seven pairs of them, each pair having charge of one day of the week, together with the planet after which it was called. Cronus and his wife Rhea kept their own day, Saturday (named for the planet Saturn), as a holiday. But the Olympian Council forbade mortals, whom Prometheus the Titan of Wednesday, had created out of river mud, ever to reckon by weeks again.

Most of the Titans and Titanesses were banished at the same time as Cronus. However, Zeus spared his aunt Metis, and his mother, Rhea, for having helped him to defeat Cronus. He also spared Prometheus for having warned his fellow-Titans that Zeus must win the war, fighting on the Olympians' side, and persuading Epimetheus to do the same. Atlas, the leader of Cronus's defeated army, was condemned by the Olympian Council to carry the Heavens on his shoulders until the end of the world.

Zeus discovered later that Prometheus had secretly entered Olympus, with Athene's guidance, and stolen a glowing coal from Hestia's hearth, so that the mortals created by him could now cook their meat, instead of eating it raw. Prometheus hid the coal in the pith of a huge fennel stalk, and carried it safely down to earth, still alight. To punish him for giving mortals this first start towards civilization, Zeus hit on a clever plan. He created a beautiful, foolish, disobedient woman whom he named Pandora, and sent her to Epimetheus as a present. When Epimetheus wanted to marry Pandora, Prometheus warned him: 'This is a trick of Zeus's. Be wise and send her back.' So Epimetheus said to Hermes, who had brought Pandora: 'Please thank Zeus very much for his kindness, but tell him that I am unworthy of such a beautiful gift and must refuse it.'

Angrier than ever, Zeus pretended that Prometheus had visited Heaven in an attempt to steal away Athene. He chained Prometheus to a rock in the Caucasus Mountains, where a vulture sat and gnawed at him all day.

Meanwhile Epimetheus, frightened by Prometheus's punishment, married Pandora. One day Pandora found a sealed jar at the back of a cupboard. It was the jar which Prometheus had asked Epimetheus to keep safely hidden and on no account to open. Though Epimetheus ordered Pandora to leave it alone, she broke the seal—as Zeus intended her to do. Out came a swarm of nasty winged things called Old Age, Sickness, Insanity, Spite, Passion, Vice, Plague, Famine, and so forth. These stung Pandora and Epimetheus most viciously, afterwards going on to attack Prometheus's mortals (who had until then lived happy, decent lives) and spoil everything for them. However, a bright-winged creature called Hope flew out of the jar last of all, and kept mortals from killing themselves in utter despair.

THE UNDERWORLD OF TARTARUS

CHAPTER FIVE

*

THE UNDERWORLD OF TARTARUS

.

Tartarus, the kingdom over which King Hades and Queen Persephone reigned, lay deep below the earth. When mortals died, Hermes ordered their souls to follow through the air, and led them to the main entrance—in a grove of black poplars beside the Western Ocean—and down by a dark tunnel to an underground river, called Styx. There they paid Charon, the old, bearded ferryman, to row them across, using the coins which relations had placed beneath the tongues of their corpses. They then became ghosts. Charon told ghosts who had no money that they must either shiver for ever on the riverbank, or else find their way back to Greece and take a side entrance at Taenarus, where admission would be free. Hades's enormous three-headed dog, named Cerberus, let no ghosts escape and prevented any live mortal from entering.

The nearest region of Tartarus consisted of the stony Asphodel Fields, over which ghosts endlessly wandered, but found nothing whatever to do except hunt the ghosts of deer—if that amused them. Asphodels are tall, pinkish-white flowers, with leaves like leeks, and roots like sweet-potatoes. Beyond these Asphodel Fields stood Hades's towering cold palace. To the left of it grew a cypress tree, marking Lethe, the Pool of Forgetfulness, where ordinary ghosts flocked thirstily to drink. At once they forgot their past lives, which left them nothing whatever to talk about. But ghosts who had been given a secret password by Orpheus, the poet, whispered it to Hades's servants, and went instead to drink from Mnemosyne, the Pool of Memory, marked by a white poplar. This allowed them to discuss their past lives, and they could also foretell the future. Hades let such ghosts make brief visits to the upper air, when their descendants wanted to ask them questions and would sacrifice a pig to him as a fee.

On their first arrival in Tartarus, ghosts were taken to be tried by the three Judges of the Dead: Minos, Rhadamanthys and Aeacus. Those whose lives had been neither very good nor very bad got sent to the Asphodel Fields; the very bad went to the Punishment Ground behind Hades's palace; the very good, to a gate near the Pool of Memory, which led to a land of orchards called Elysium. Elysium basked in perpetual sunshine; games, music, and fun went on there without a stop; flowers never faded; and every sort of fruit was always in season. The lucky ghosts sent to Elysium might visit the earth, unsummoned, every All Souls' Night, and whoever pleased might then creep inside a bean, hoping that some kind, healthy, rich girl would eat it; he would be later born as her baby. This explains why no decent man in those days ate beans: fearing to swallow the ghost of one of his parents or grandparents.

Hades grew immensely rich because of all the gold and silver and jewels that lie underground; yet everyone hated him, including Persephone, who pitied the poor ghosts in his charge and had no children of her own to console her. Hades's most valuable possession was a helmet of invisibility, made by the one-eyed Cyclopes when they were sent down to Tartarus by Cronus. As soon as Cronus had been banished, Hades released the Cyclopes at Zeus's orders, and they gave him the helmet in gratitude.

The Three Furies took charge of the Punishment Ground: horrible, withered, savage, coal-black women with snakes for hair, faces like dogs', wings like bats', and burning eyes; they carried torches and cat-o'-nine-tail whips. The Furies often visited the earth, too, to punish living mortals who behaved cruelly to children, or rudely to old people and guests, or unkindly to beggars; and hounded to death anyone who treated his mother badly, however wicked she might have been. Among the famous criminals on the Punishment Ground were the forty-nine Danaids. Their father, Danaus, the King of Argos, had been forced to marry them to their forty-nine cousins, sons of his brother Aegyptus. Danaus secretly gave the Danaids long, sharp pins, which he told them to stick in their husbands' hearts on the common wedding night. The Danaids obeyed and, when at last they died, were not whipped by the Furies, because after all they had only obeyed their father's orders, but condemned to fetch water in jars from the River Styx and fill Hades's garden pond. The jars were holed at the bottom, like sieves, so the Danaids trudged endlessly to and fro, from the river to the pond and back again, never finishing their task. (A fiftieth Danaid, called Hypermnestra, had also been given a long, sharp pin, but happened to fall in love with her husband and helped him to escape unhurt. Hypermnestra went straight to Elysium when she died.)

Tantalus of Lydia was another criminal. He stole ambrosia, the food of the gods, to share among his mortal friends, and then (as though this were not bad enough) invited the Olympians to a banquet and offered them cannibal stew, made from the body of his murdered nephew Pelops! The Olympians at once recognized the meat as human. Zeus killed Tantalus with a thunderbolt, and restored Pelops to life. Down in Tartarus, Minos, Rhadamanthys, and Aeacus tied Tantalus to a fruit tree, beside the River Styx, on which grew pears, apples, figs, and pomegranates, but whenever he tried to pick any of the fruit that dangled against his shoulders, a wind always swept the branch away. Moreover, the river water lapped against Tantalus's waist, but whenever he bent to drink, it always sank out of reach. He suffered endless agony from hunger and thirst.

Sisyphus of Corinth had once betrayed a secret of Zeus's. The Judges condemned him to roll a huge stone up the side of a hill and tumble it over the farther slope. As soon as he got the stone almost to the top, it never failed to bound down with mighty leaps, and he had to begin all over again, exhausted though he was by his continual efforts.

THE BIRTH OF HERMES

CHAPTER SIX

*

THE BIRTH OF HERMES

As soon as Hermes had been born in an Arcadian cave, his mother, Maia, bustled about lighting a fire to heat some water for his first bath, while Cyllene, the nurse, took a pitcher to fill at the nearest stream. Being a god, Hermes grew within a few minutes to the size of a four-year-old boy, climbed out of his basket cradle, and tiptoed away in search of adventure. He was tempted to steal a fine herd of Apollo's own cows. To disguise their tracks, he made them shoes from bark and plaited grass, then drove the herd into a wood behind the cave, where he tied them to trees. Apollo missed the cows, and offered a reward for discovery of the thief. Silenus, Pan's son, who lived not far off with his friends the Satyrs—half goats, half men, like himself and his father— joined the search. As he came near Maia's cave, Silenus heard wonderful music coming from inside.

He stopped and, seeing Cyllene in the cave mouth, called out to her: 'Who is that musician?'

Cyllene answered: 'A clever little boy, born only yesterday. He's made a new sort of musical instrument by stringing cow-gut tight across the hollow shell of a tortoise.'

Silenus noticed two newly flayed white cowhides pegged down to dry. 'Did the gut come from the same cows as these hides?' he asked.

'Do you accuse the innocent child of theft?'

'Certainly! Either your gifted child has stolen Apollo's white cows, or else you have.'

'How dare you say such things, you nasty old man? And, please, keep your voice low, or you'll wake the child's mother.'

At that moment Apollo flew down, and went straight into the cave, muttering: 'I know by my magic that the thief is here.' He woke Maia. 'Madam, your son has stolen my cows. He must give them up at once!'

Maia yawned. 'What a ridiculous charge! My son is only just born.'

'These are hides from my precious white cows,' said Apollo. 'Come along, you bad boy!'

He caught hold of Hermes, who was pretending to be asleep, and carried him to Olympus, where he called a council of the gods and accused him of theft.

Zeus frowned, and asked: 'Who are you, little boy?'

'Your son Hermes, Father,' Hermes answered. 'I was born yesterday.'

'Then you certainly must be innocent of this crime.'

'You know best, Father.'

'He stole my cows,' said Apollo.

'I was too young to know right from wrong yesterday,' explained Hermes. 'Today I do, and I beg your pardon. You may have the rest of those cows, if they are yours. I killed only two, and cut them up into twelve equal portions for sacrifice to the twelve gods.'

'Twelve gods? Who is the twelfth?' asked Apollo.

'Myself,' said Hermes, bowing politely.

They went together to the cave, where Hermes took the tortoise-shell lyre from under the blankets of his cradle and played so beautifully on it that Apollo exclaimed: 'Hand over that instrument. *I* am the God of Music!'

'Very well, if I may keep your cows,' said Hermes.

They shook hands on the bargain, the first ever made, and returning to Olympus told Zeus that the affair had been settled.

Zeus sat Hermes on his knee. 'Now, my son, be careful in the future neither to steal nor to tell lies. You seem to be a clever little boy. You arranged matters with Apollo very well.'

'Then make me your herald, Father,' begged Hermes. 'I promise never again to tell lies, though sometimes it may be best not to tell the whole truth.'

'So be it. And you shall take charge of all treaties and all buying and selling, and protect the right of travellers to go down any public road they please, so long as they behave peaceably.'

Zeus then gave Hermes his peeled wand and the white ribbons; also a golden hat against the rain; and winged golden sandals to make him fly faster than the wind.

Besides the letters of the alphabet (with which, by the way, the Three Fates helped him), Hermes also invented arithmetic, astronomy, musical scales, weights and measures, the art of boxing, and gymnastics.

The Sun, whose name was Helius, owned a palace near Colchis in the Far East beyond the Black Sea. He counted among the smaller gods, because his father had been a Titan. At cockcrow every morning, Helius harnessed four white horses to a fiery chariot—so bright that nobody could look at it without hurting his eyes—which he drove across the sky to another palace in the Far West, near the Elysian Fields. There he unharnessed his team, and when they had grazed, loaded them and the chariot on a golden ferryboat, in which he sailed, fast asleep, round the world by way of the Ocean Stream until he reached Colchis again. Helius

43

enjoyed watching what went on in the world below, but he could never take a holiday from work.

Phaëthon, his eldest son, was constantly asking permission to drive the chariot. 'Why not have a day in bed for a change, Father?' Helius always answered: 'I must wait until you are a little older.' Phaëthon grew so impatient and bad-tempered—throwing stones at the Palace windows, and pulling up the flowers in the garden—that at last Helius said: 'Very well, then, you may drive it tomorrow. But keep a firm hold of the reins. The horses are very spirited.' Phaëthon tried to show off before his younger sisters, and the horses, realizing that he did not know how to manage the reins, started plunging up and down. The Olympians felt icy cold one minute, and the next saw trees and grasses scorching from the heat. 'Stop those stupid tricks, boy!' shouted Zeus.

'My team is out of control, Your Majesty,' gasped Phaëthon.

Zeus, in disgust, threw a thunderbolt at Phaëthon, and killed him. His body fell into the River Po. The little girls wept and wept. Zeus changed them to poplar trees.

Helius had a sister named Eos, or Dawn, who got out of bed every morning just before the Sun, mounted another chariot (a rose-coloured one), and went to tell the Olympians that her brother was on the way. Dawn married a mortal named Tithonus, whom Zeus made immortal for her sake; but she forgot to ask that he might always stay young. Tithonus grew older and older, greyer and greyer, uglier and uglier, smaller and smaller, until he ended as a grass-hopper.

ORPHEUS

CHAPTER SEVEN

*

ORPHEUS

Orpheus's mother was Calliope, one of the Nine Muses, and she inspired poets. Besides being a poet, Orpheus played the lyre so well that he could not only tame wild beasts with his music, but make rocks and trees move from their places to follow him. One unlucky day his beautiful wife Eurydice trod on a sleeping snake, which woke and bit her. She died of the poison, so Orpheus boldly went down to Tartarus, playing his lyre, to fetch her away. He charmed Charon into ferrying him across the Styx without payment; he charmed Cerberus into whining and licking his feet; he charmed the Furies into laying down their whips and listening to him, while all punishments ceased; he charmed Queen Persephone into giving him the secret password for the Pool of Memory; he even charmed King Hades into freeing Eurydice and letting her follow him up on earth again. Hades made only one condition: that Orpheus must not look behind him until Eurydice was safely back in the sunlight. So he went off, singing and playing happily. Eurydice followed; but at the last minute Orpheus feared that Hades might be tricking him, forgot the condition, looked anxiously behind him—and lost her forever.

When Zeus made his son Dionysus an Olympian, Orpheus refused to worship the new god, whom he accused of setting mortals a bad example by his wild behaviour.

Dionysus angrily ordered a crowd of Maenads—drunken young women—to chase Orpheus. They caught him without his lyre, cut off his head, which they threw into a river, and tore him into little pieces. The Nine Muses sadly collected these and buried them at the foot of Mount Olympus, where the nightingales ever afterwards sang more sweetly than anywhere else. Orpheus's head floated singing down the river to the sea, and fishermen rescued it for burial on the island of Lemnos. Zeus then let Apollo put Orpheus's lyre in the sky as the constellation still called the Lyre.

DEUCALION'S FLOOD

CHAPTER EIGHT

*

DEUCALION'S FLOOD

Once, when Zeus walked on earth disguised as a poor traveller, he found the people of Arcadia behaving so cruelly and
unkindly that he decided to wipe out all mortals with an
enormous flood. At the same time Deucalion, King of Phthia,
visited his father Prometheus in the Caucasus and tried to
drive off the vulture that was feeding on him, but it always
came back. Prometheus, who could foresee the future,
warned Deucalion of the flood; so Deucalion built himself
an ark, filled it with his flocks, herds, and other possessions,
and hurried aboard. His wife, Pyrrha, came too. Then the
South Wind blew, rain fell in sheets, the rivers rushed down
the mountainsides, washing away cities and temples and
drowning living creatures. The ark floated high over the
trees, and still the water went on rising. At last only a few
mountain peaks still stood above water. Presently the rain
ceased, and the ark, after tossing about for nine days, came
to rest at the top of Mount Othrys in Thessaly, not far from
Phthia. Deucalion and Pyrrha climbed out, sacrificed a ram
to Zeus and, as soon as the flood subsided a little, found a
temple covered with seaweed and wreckage, where they
sadly prayed that mankind might be spared. Zeus heard their
prayer, and sent Hermes to tell them: 'All will be well. Cover
your heads and throw the bones of your mother behind you.'
Since Deucalion and Pyrrha had different mothers, both

of them buried in graveyards now deep under water, they guessed that 'your mother' meant Mother Earth. Covering their heads, they threw stones behind them. The stones turned into men and women on touching the ground.

A few other mortals had also been saved. Parnassus, a son of the God Poseidon, was woken by the sound of wolves yelping for fear, and followed them to the top of a mountain now called after him. And Megarus, a son of Zeus, was woken by the screaming of cranes, and followed them to the top of Mount Gerania. Both these survivors brought their families with them to safety.

ORION

CHAPTER NINE

*

ORION

Orion of Boeotia, the handsomest man and the cleverest hunter alive, fell in love with Merope, daughter of Oenopion, King of Chios. 'You may marry Merope,' Oenopion said, 'if you promise to kill all the wild beasts of my island.' This Orion did, and every evening took the skins of dead bears, lions, wolves, wildcats, and foxes to Merope at the palace. When he had cleared Chios of all wild animals larger than mice and weasels, he knocked on Oenopion's door. 'Now let me marry your daughter.'

'Not so,' Oenopion answered. 'At dawn this morning I heard wolves howling, lions and bears roaring, foxes barking, and wildcats mewing. You have not yet nearly finished your task.'

Orion went away and got drunk. That night he broke into Merope's bedroom. 'Come to the Temple of Aphrodite and marry me!' he shouted. Merope screamed for help, and Oenopion, afraid of getting hurt if he interfered, hurriedly sent along a pack of satyrs to give Orion still more wine to drink.

'Here's to a happy marriage!' the satyrs cried. Orion thanked them, drank a great deal, and fell to the ground in a stupor. Then the cruel Oenopion crept up and put out both his eyes. But Orion, though blind, heard a Cyclops hammering in the distance, and followed the sound to a

forge. There he borrowed the Cyclops's boy as his guide
to the farthest East, where the Sun stabled his horses beside
the Ocean for his daily ride across the sky. The Sun took
pity on Orion and restored his sight. Orion went back to
Chios for vengeance. Oenopion, warned of his arrival, hid
in a tomb and told the servants to say that he had gone
abroad; so Orion visited Crete in search of him. The Goddess Artemis, who happened to be about, welcomed Orion.
'Why not let us go hunting together,' she asked, 'and see who
can kill most wild goats?'

'I am no match for a goddess like yourself,' answered
Orion politely, 'but I should dearly love to watch you shoot.'

The God Apollo, Artemis's brother, heard of this engage-
ment and muttered angrily: 'I fear she has fallen in love
with this mortal. I must put a stop to it.' He sent an enormous
scorpion, bigger than an elephant, to attack Orion. Orion
shot the scorpion full of arrows, and then used his sword;
but, being unable to kill the monster, dived into the sea and
swam off. Apollo told Artemis, who had just arrived with
bow and arrows: 'Do you see that black thing bobbing up
and down far out to sea?'

'I do,' answered Artemis.

'That's the head of a wretch called Candaon,' said Apollo.
'He has insulted one of your priestesses. Kill him!'

Artemis believed Apollo, took careful aim, and shot. Dis-
covering that she had killed Orion, she turned him into a
constellation, eternally pursued by a scorpion—to remind
everyone of Apollo's jealousy and lies.

ASCLEPIUS

CHAPTER TEN

ASCLEPIUS

Artemis revenged herself on Apollo for the death of Orion by shooting Coronis, a Thessalian woman whom he had married. But she let their baby be born alive. Apollo named the boy Asclepius, and carried him to Mount Pelion, nearby, where Cheiron, King of the Centaurs, took charge of his education.

The Centaurs were half men, half horses, and very wise; their worst fault being a habit of getting drunk at weddings and breaking all the furniture. Cheiron acted as tutor to some of the bravest heroes on earth, including Heracles and Jason. He taught Asclepius archery, and the alphabet, and astronomy, though finding him most interested in medicines. After several years at Cheiron's school, Asclepius became the best doctor in Greece. Not only did he cure dying people, but on three or four occasions restored dead men to life, using a magical herb which had been shown him by a snake in a tomb.

King Hades complained to Zeus: 'One of Apollo's sons is stealing my subjects.'

'Come, come,' Zeus answered, 'Asclepius does these cures out of the goodness of his heart. Can I blame him? Anyhow, all his patients die sooner or later, so why are you cross?'

'You are wrong,' said Hades, 'he does his cures for money. The other day he revived King Lycurgus, whose body was torn into pieces by wild horses at your son Dionysus's orders. Lycurgus, you remember, had defeated Dionysus's army as it came back in triumph from India. The royal family paid Asclepius a lapful of gold for what he did.'

'Oh, very well, then,' grunted Zeus. He threw a thunderbolt at Asclepius and killed him, just to please Dionysus.

Asclepius's death enraged Apollo. He revenged himself by shooting dead all the Cyclopes, who had built the walls of Olympus and forged Zeus's thunderbolts as well.

Zeus punished Apollo by ordering him to become a common herdsman for a year, in the service of King Admetus of Pherae, a mere mortal.

KING MIDAS'S EARS

*

CHAPTER ELEVEN

KING MIDAS'S EARS

Midas, a pleasure-loving King of Macedonia, planted the first rose garden in the world, and spent all his days feasting and listening to music. One morning his gardeners complained: A drunken old satyr is entangled in your best rose bush.'

'Bring the wretch here,' said Midas.

The satyr proved to be Silenus, who had gone to India and back as Dionysus's tutor. He told Midas exciting stories about India, and about a new continent lying across the Atlantic, where tall, happy, long-lived mortals inhabited wonderful cities; and how these giants had once sailed to Europe in hundreds of ships, but thought everything there so dull and ugly that they soon sailed home again.

Midas entertained Silenus for five days and nights, listening to these stories, and then sent him safe to Dionysus. Dionysus gratefully promised to grant Midas any wish he pleased; and Midas chose the magic power of transforming into gold whatever he touched. It was great fun at first: making gold roses and golden nightingales out of the ordinary ones. Then, by mistake, he turned his own daughter into a statue, and also found that the food he ate and the wine he drank were turning to gold in his mouth; so that he nearly died of hunger and thirst. Dionysus laughed loudly at Midas, but let him wash off the 'golden touch' in the

Phrygian river Pactolus—the sands of which are still bright with gold—and restore his daughter, too. He also helped him to become King of Phrygia.

One day Apollo asked Midas to judge a musical competition between himself and a Phrygian shepherd named Marsyas. This is how it came about. The Goddess Athene had invented the double flute, made from stags' bones, and played enchanting tunes on it at a banquet of the Olympians. But Hera and Aphrodite began to giggle, and Athene could not guess why. So she went to Phrygia and played the flute all by herself, watching her reflection in a woodland stream. When she saw how silly her puffed cheeks and red face made her look, she threw away the flute, with a curse on anyone who picked it up. Marsyas happened to find the flute, and when he put it to his lips, such wonderful tunes flowed out that he challenged Apollo to this competition.

Apollo ordered the Muses and Midas to act as judges. When Marsyas played the flute, and Apollo the lyre, the judges could not at first agree which had given the best performance. Apollo then told Marsyas: 'In that case, I challenge you to play your instrument upside-down, as I do mine.' So saying, he turned the lyre upside-down, and played almost as well as before. Since Marsyas could not, of course, do the same with his flute, the Muses announced: 'Apollo wins.'

'No, that was an unfair test,' said Midas.

However, the Muses were against him, nine to one, and Apollo told Marsyas: 'You must die, miserable mortal, for daring to challenge the God of Music himself!' He shot Marsyas through the heart, flayed him, and gave his skin to the satyrs for making drums.

Then he called Midas an ass, and touched his ears, which sprouted up, long and hairy, like an ass's. Midas blushed, covered them with a tall Phrygian cap, and begged the Muses not to talk about the matter. Unfortunately Midas's barber had to know, because Phrygians cut their hair very short; but Midas threatened to kill him if he told a living creature. The barber, bursting with the secret, dug a hole in the bank of the Pactolus river, looked carefully around, for fear anyone might be listening, and then whispered into the hole: 'King Midas has ass's ears.' He filled up the hole at once to bury the secret, and went away happy. But a reed sprouted from the hole and whispered to the other reeds: 'King Midas has ass's ears; King Midas has ass's ears!' Soon the birds got hold of the news and brought it to a man named Melampus, who understood their language. Melampus told his friends, and at last Midas, driving out in his chariot, heard all his people shouting in chorus: 'Remove that cap, King Midas! We want to see your ears!' Midas first cut off the barber's head, and then killed himself for shame.

MELAMPUS AND PHYLACUS

CHAPTER TWELVE

*

MELAMPUS AND PHYLACUS

One day Melampus of Pylus prevented his servants from killing a brood of snakes, whose mother had been run over by a cart. In gratitude, the little snakes wriggled into his bed while he slept and licked his ears with their forked tongues. Melampus woke up and found that he could understand the language of birds and insects. Though disappointed to find how dull their conversations usually were, he sometimes overheard most interesting secrets.

Bias, Melampus's twin brother, wanted to marry their cousin Pero; but Pero's father would not agree unless Bias promised to give him a prize-winning herd of cows that belonged to a bad-tempered old neighbour. This neighbour, whose name was Phylacus, refused to sell at any price, and Bias nearly died of disappointment. However, Melampus overheard two cranes chatting together as they caught frogs in the pond near his home. One said: 'What a pity about Bias and those cows, eh?'

'Yes,' answered the other, 'but I happen to know that whoever tried to steal them, except Bias himself, will go to prison for exactly a year, and then be given them as a present. If Bias tries, Phylacus is fated to kill him. Oh, what a beautiful fat frog!'

To help Bias, Melampus stole the cows, got caught by Phylacus, and was shut up in his private prison.

Ten nights before the end of his year as a prisoner, Melampus heard a pair of wood-worms talking in the beam above his head. One remarked that if they ate at the wood really hard all night, it would collapse at dawn the next day. Melampus hammered on the door of his cell and demanded to be taken into another one.

'Why?' asked Phylacus.

'Because this beam is going to collapse at dawn. If it kills me, the gods will punish you for not doing as I say.'

'Nonsense!'

'No, it is the truth.'

Just before dawn Phylacus thought that he had better put Melampus into another cell. He did so, and then sent a slave-woman to fetch Melampus's bed. She was lugging it out when the beam fell and killed her.

Phylacus was astonished. 'You seem to be a prophet, my lord Melampus,' he said. 'Perhaps you can help me. My son has been paralysed since childhood. If you tell me how to cure him, I promise to give you my prize-winning herd of cows, and your freedom too.'

Melampus sacrificed a bull to Apollo, taking care to leave the insides lying beside the altar for the vultures to eat. Vultures, like cranes, are prophetic birds, and soon two flew down. As one tore at the offal with his hooked beak, Melampus heard him say: 'This is my first feed here since the day ten years ago, when Phylacus sacrificed that ram to Zeus. I remember how his cowardly little boy screamed on seeing him take up his knife and kill the ram. Phylacus ran to comfort the boy, first sticking the knife into that pear tree over there for safety. Afterwards he forgot to pull it out again. That annoyed the Goddess Hera, to whom pear trees are sacred. She paralysed the boy as a punishment. Look, the knife is still where Phylacus left it, nearly overgrown by bark.'

The other vulture answered, with its mouth full: 'If Phylacus only had the sense to pull out the knife, scrape off the rust, mix it with water, and give the drink to his son, morning and night, for ten days, that would completely cure the paralysis.'

Melampus passed on the vulture's advice to Phylacus, who sacrificed a lamb, praying aloud for Hera's forgiveness, and in ten days cured his son with the rusty water.

Phylacus gave Melampus the cows. Melampus gave them to Bias. Bias gave them to Pero's father. Pero's father gave Pero to Bias. Bias thanked Melampus as the best of brothers; and all ended happily, for once.

EUROPA AND CADMUS

*

CHAPTER THIRTEEN

EUROPA AND CADMUS

Agenor the Egyptian settled in Palestine long before the
time of Moses, and had five sons and one daughter, by name
Europa. One fine day Zeus, looking down from Olympus,
fell in love with Europa. He disguised himself as a snow-
white bull, and gambolled about on the seashore near Agen-
or's city of Tyre. The bull looked so tame that Europa went
up to pat him, and presently fetched a basketful of flowers
which she wreathed around his horns. Then she kissed his
nose, climbed on his strong back, and went for a ride along
the shore. Suddenly he waded into the water and swam away
with her. Europa feared to let go of his horns, being a very
poor swimmer, and her maids of honour stood helpless,
watching their lovely princess disappear in the distance.

Agenor told his five sons to go in search of Europa, and
not to return without her. None of them succeeded in finding her, because Zeus had put a curse on any god or mortal
who revealed that he had swum across to Crete, and married
her there. The eldest son, Phineus, went as far as the shores
of the Black Sea, gave up the search, and made his home
near the Bosporus. Cilix, the next, settled in Cilicia (since
called after him), and became a pirate. Thasus stopped on
the island of Thasus, and mined for gold. Phoenix visited
Africa, where he founded cities, but eventually, after Agen-
or's death, returned to Palestine, part of which is called

'Phoenicia' after him. Cadmus, the youngest of the five, went to Greece, and asked Apollo's oracle at Delphi where Europa had gone. Apollo's priestess answered: 'Be wise, Cadmus, and give up your search. Instead, follow a cow with a white full-moon on each haunch. When she lies down, sacrifice her to Athene, and build a city.'

Cadmus soon saw just such a cow. He and his companions followed her all the way to Boeotia before she lay down. Then he said: 'We must sprinkle her with holy water for sacrifice. Fetch a helmetful from that spring!'

The spring belonged to Ares, God of War, who kept a huge dragon as its guardian. When the dragon killed Cadmus's men, he went himself and crushed its head with a rock. Athene, sniffing the pleasant smell of roast cow, flew down from Olympus, thanked him, and said: 'Pull out all these dragon's teeth, and sow them as if they were seeds!'

Cadmus obeyed and, to his surprise, the teeth sprouted up into armed men.

'Now throw a stone at them!' Athene ordered.

He obeyed again, hiding behind a rock; and at once the armed men began accusing one another of having thrown it. A fight started, at the end of which only five men were left, all wounded. Cadmus bandaged their wounds and cared for them until they recovered. Then they gratefully swore to obey him both in peace and in war. He set them to build the famous city of Thebes.

When Ares complained that his pet dragon had been cruelly killed, the Council of Olympians sentenced Cadmus to be Ares's servant for ninety-nine months; but at the end, after helping Ares in several wars, he was set free and ruled peaceably over Thebes.

Meanwhile Europa became the mother, by her marriage to Zeus, of Minos and Rhadamanthys, later the Judges of the Dead; and gave her name to the continent of Europe.

DAEDALUS

CHAPTER FOURTEEN

*

DAEDALUS

Daedalus, the Athenian, a wonderfully skilful smith taught by Athene and Hephaestus, grew jealous of his nephew Talus and killed him. Talus, though only twelve years old, had invented the saw, which he copied in brass from the teeth of a snake. To avoid being hanged, Daedalus fled to Crete, where King Minos, Europa's son, welcomed him. Minos was short of good workmen. Daedalus married a Cretan girl, by whom he had a son named Icarus; and made Minos all sorts of statues, furniture, machines, weapons, armour, and toys for the palace children. After some years he asked for a month's holiday, and when Minos said: 'Certainly not!' decided to escape.

He knew it would be useless to steal a boat and sail away, because Minos's fast ships would soon overtake him. So he made himself and Icarus a pair of wings each, to strap on their arms. The big quills he threaded to a frame; but the smaller feathers were held together by bees-wax. Having helped Icarus on with his pair of wings, Daedalus warned him: 'Be careful not to fly too low, my boy, for fear of the sea spray; or too high, for fear of the sun.'

Daedalus flew off, Icarus followed; but presently soared so near the sun that the wax melted and the feathers came unstuck. Icarus lost height, fell into the sea and drowned.

Daedalus buried his son's body on a small island, later

called Icaria, where the sea had washed it up; then sadly flew on to the court of King Cocalus in Sicily. Minos pursued him by ship, but Daedalus begged the Sicilians not to reveal his hiding place. However, the clever Minos took a large triton shell, and offered a bag of gold to anyone who could pass a linen thread through all the shell's whorls, and out through a tiny hole at the very top. When he came to Cocalus's palace, Cocalus, anxious to win the reward, took the shell indoors and asked Daedalus to solve the problem for him. 'That is easy,' said Daedalus. 'Tie the gossamer from a spider's web to the hind-leg of an ant, put the ant into the shell, and then smear honey around the hole at the top. The ant will smell the honey and go circling up all the whorls in search of it. As soon as the ant reappears, catch it, tie a woman's hair to the other end of the gossamer, and pull it carefully through. Then tie a linen thread to the end of the hair, and pull that through as well.'

Cocalus followed his advice. Minos, seeing the threaded shell, paid him the gold, but said sternly: 'Only Daedalus could have thought of this! I shall burn your palace to the ground, unless you give him up.'

Cocalus promised to do so, and invited Minos to take a warm bath in the new bathroom built by Daedalus. But Cocalus's daughters, to save their friend—who had given them a set of beautiful dolls, with movable arms and legs—poured boiling water down the bathroom pipe instead of warm, and scalded Minos to death. Cocalus pretended that Minos had died by accident: tripping over the bath-mat and falling into the tub before cold water could be added. Fortunately the Cretans believed this story.

BELLEROPHON

CHAPTER FIFTEEN

*

BELLEROPHON

Bellerophon of Corinth was engaged to marry the princess Aethra, but accidentally killed a man in a dart-throwing competition and had to leave the country. He fled to the town of Tiryns, where the King invited him to be his guest. The Queen fell in love with Bellerophon, caught hold of him on the stairs, and said: 'Darling, let us run away together!'

'Certainly not!' exclaimed Bellerophon. 'You are married, and the King has been very kind to me.'

The Queen went to the King and whispered spitefully in his ear: 'That rascal Bellerophon has just asked me to run away with him. Did you ever hear of such shocking behaviour?'

The King believed the story, but dared not offend the Furies by killing his guest. Instead, he wrote a letter to his father-in-law Iobates, the King of Lycia in Asia Minor, and sent Bellerophon across the sea with it. The letter, which was sealed, read: 'Please behead the bearer of this. He has been very rude to my Queen, your daughter.'

King Iobates dared not offend Hermes, the God of Travellers and Messengers, by beheading Bellerophon. Instead, he asked him to kill the Chimaera. This Chimaera was a fire-breathing goat with a lion's head and snake's tail, which guarded the palace of Iobates's enemy, the King of Caria.

Bellerophon promised to do his best. He prayed to the Goddess Athene, who advised him first to tame a wild winged horse called Pegasus, living on Mount Helicon, which the Muses fed in winter when snow covered the grass. Bellerophon knew that Pegasus often flew south to the Isthmus of Corinth; and had once or twice seen him drinking at a favourite spring there. So Bellerophon revisited Corinth in secret—being afraid that he might be arrested for murder; and prayed to Athene again. Athene brought him a golden bridle, with which he waited all night behind a rock near the spring, until at dawn, by good luck, Pegasus flew down to drink. Quickly Bellerophon threw the bridle over Pegasus's head, and tamed him after a fierce struggle.

At that moment, Bellerophon's enemies came up to arrest him; but he mounted Pegasus and flew away to Caria. There he circled above the palace until he saw the Chimaera blowing fire in the courtyard beneath, and shot her full of arrows. But he could not kill the monster, until he stuck a lump of lead on the point of a spear and pushed it into her open jaws. The fiery breath melted the lead: it trickled down her throat and burned holes in her stomach. So died the Chimaera.

Afterwards, Iobates gave Bellerophon several other important tasks. Bellerophon behaved with such courage and modesty on every occasion, that at last Iobates showed him the letter from Tiryns, and said: 'Tell me, is this true?' When Bellerophon explained what had really happened, Iobates cried: 'There! My eldest daughter was always a liar, and I apologize for believing the story.' Then he married Bellerophon to his younger daughter, who was both well-behaved and beautiful, and in his will left him the throne of Lycia.

Bellerophon grew very proud. He stupidly tried to call on

the Olympians in their palace, without having been invited. He rode through the air on Pegasus, dressed in crown and robes. Zeus, seeing him from a long way off, shouted: 'A curse on this impudent mortal! Hera, my dear, please send a gadfly to sting Pegasus under the tail!' Hera did so. Pegasus reared, and Bellerophon tumbled off. He fell half a mile, bounced off the side of a river valley, and rolled down a slope into a thorn bush. After that, his fate was to wander about the earth under Zeus's curse: lame, poor, and deserted by his friends. But Zeus caught Pegasus and used him as a pack-horse to carry thunderbolts.

THESEUS

CHAPTER SIXTEEN

*

THESEUS

On a visit to Corinth, King Aegeus of Athens secretly married the Princess Aethra. She had grown tired of waiting for Bellerophon, whose wife she should have been, to come home from Lydia. After a few pleasant days with Aethra, Aegeus told her: 'I am afraid I must leave now, my dear. It will be safest, in case you have a son, to pretend that his father is the God Poseidon. My eldest nephew might kill you if he knew of our marriage. He expects to be the next King of Athens. Goodbye!'

Once back, Aegeus never left Athens again.

Aethra had a son whom she named Theseus, and on his fourteenth birthday she asked him: 'Can you move that huge rock?' Theseus, a remarkably strong boy, lifted the rock and tossed it away. Hidden underneath, he found a sword with a golden snake pattern inlaid on the blade, and a pair of sandals. 'Those were left there by your father,' Aethra said. 'He is Aegeus, King of Athens. Take them to him and say that you found them under this rock. But mind, not a word to his nephews, who will be furious if they discover that you are the true heir to the throne of Athens. Because of them I have pretended all these years that Poseidon, not Aegeus, was your father.'

Theseus went by the coast road to Athens. First he met a giant named Sinis, who had the horrible habit of bending two pine trees down towards each other, tying some poor traveller to their tops by his arms, and then suddenly letting go. The trees would fly upright and tear him in two. Theseus wrestled with Sinis, threw him senseless on the ground, and then treated him as he had treated others.

Next, Theseus faced and killed a monstrous wild sow, with tusks larger and sharper than sickles. Then he fought Procrustes, a wicked innkeeper who lived beside the main road and kept only one bed in his inn. If travellers were too short for the bed, Procrustes would lengthen them with an instrument of torture called 'the rack'; if they were too tall, he would chop off their feet; and if they were the right size, he would smother them with a blanket. Theseus beat Procrustes, tied him to the bed, and cut off both his feet; but, finding him still too tall, cut off his head as well. He wrapped the dead body in a blanket and flung it into the sea.

King Aegeus had recently been married again: to a witch named Medea. Theseus did not know about this marriage, yet on his arrival at Athens, Medea knew by magic who he was; and decided to poison him—putting wolfbane in a cup of wine. She wanted one of her own sons to be the next King. Luckily Aegeus noticed the snake pattern on Theseus's sword, guessed that the wine had been poisoned, and hastily knocked the cup from Medea's hand. The poison burned a large hole through the floor, and Medea escaped in a magic cloud. Then Aegeus sent a chariot to fetch Aethra from Corinth, and announced: 'Theseus is my son and heir.' The next day, Aegeus's nephews ambushed Theseus on his way to a temple; but he fought and killed them all.

Now, it had happened some years before that King Minos's son, Androgeus of Crete, visited Athens and there won all the competitions in the Athletic Games—running, jumping, boxing, wrestling, and throwing the discus.

Aegeus's jealous nephews accused him of a plot to seize the throne, and murdered him. When Minos complained about this to the Olympians, they gave orders that Aegeus must send seven boys and seven girls from Athens every ninth year to be devoured by the Cretan Minotaur. The Minotaur was a monster—half bull, half man—which Minos kept in the middle of the Labyrinth, or maze, built for him by Daedalus. The Minotaur knew every twist and turn in the Labyrinth, and would chase his victims into some blind alley where he had them at his mercy.

So now the Athenians, angry with Theseus for killing his cousins, chose him as one of the seven boys sent to be eaten that year. Theseus thanked them, saying that he was glad of a chance to free his country of this horrid tribute. The ship in which the victims sailed carried black sails, for mourning, but Theseus took white sails along, too. 'If I kill the Minotaur, I shall hoist these white sails. If the Minotaur kills me, let the black ones be hoisted.'

Theseus prayed to the Goddess Aphrodite. She listened to him and told her son Eros to make Ariadne, Minos's daughter, fall in love with Theseus. That same night, she came to Theseus's prison, drugged the guards, unlocked the door of his cell with a key stolen from Minos's belt, and asked Theseus: 'If I help you to kill the Minotaur, will you marry me?'

'With pleasure,' he answered, kissing her hand.

Ariadne led the boys quietly from the prison. She showed them a magic ball of thread, given her by Daedalus before he left Crete. One need only tie the loose end of the thread to the Labyrinth door, and the ball would roll by itself through all the twisting paths until it reached the clear space in the middle. 'The Minotaur lives there,' Ariadne said. 'He

sleeps for exactly one hour in the twenty-four, at midnight; but then he sleeps sound.'

Theseus's six companions kept guard at the entrance, while Ariadne tied the thread to the Labyrinth door. Theseus entered, ran his hand along the thread in the darkness and came upon the sleeping Minotaur just after midnight. As the moon rose, he cut off the monster's head with a razor-sharp sword lent him by Ariadne, then followed the thread back to the entrance where his friends stood anxiously waiting. Meanwhile, Ariadne had freed the seven girls, too, and all together they stole down to the harbour. Theseus and his friends, having first bored holes in the sides of Minos's ships, climbed aboard their own, pushed her off, and sailed for Athens. The Cretan ships which gave chase soon filled and sank; so Theseus got safely away, with the Minotaur's head and Ariadne.

Theseus beached his ship on the island of Naxos; he needed food and water. While Ariadne lay resting on the beach, the God Dionysus suddenly appeared to Theseus. 'I want to marry this woman myself,' he said. 'If you take her from me, I will destroy Athens by sending all its people mad.'

Theseus dared not offend Dionysus and, since he had no great love for Ariadne anyway, he left her asleep and set sail. Ariadne wept with rage on waking, to find herself deserted; but Dionysus soon walked up, introduced himself, and offered her a large cup of wine. Ariadne drank it all, felt better at once, and decided that it would be far more glorious to marry a god than a mortal. Dionysus's wedding present to her was the splendid jewelled coronet which is now the constellation called 'The Northern Crown.' She bore several children to Dionysus, and eventually returned to Crete as Queen.

80

In the excitement, Theseus had quite forgotten to change the sails, and King Aegeus, watching anxiously from a cliff at Athens, saw the black sail appear instead of the white. Overcome by grief, he jumped into the sea and drowned. Theseus then became King of Athens and made peace with the Cretans.

A few years later, the Amazons, a fierce race of fighting women from Asia, invaded Greece and attacked Athens. Since Theseus listened to the Goddess Athene's advice, he managed to defeat them; but never afterwards stopped boasting about his courage.

One day his friend Peirithous said to him: 'I am in love with a beautiful woman. Will you help me to marry her?'

'By all means,' Theseus answered. 'Am I not the bravest king alive? Look what I did to the Amazons! Look what I did to the Minotaur! Who is the woman?'

'Persephone, Demeter's daughter,' Peirithous answered.

'Oh! Are you serious? Persephone is already married to King Hades, God of the Dead!'

'I know, but she hates Hades and wants children. She can have no living children by the God of the Dead.'

'It seems rather a risky adventure,' said Theseus, turning pale.

'Are you not the bravest king alive?'

'I am.'

'Let us go, then!'

They buckled on their swords and descended to Tartarus by the side entrance. Having given the dog Cerberus three cakes dipped in poppy juice, to send him asleep, Peirithous rapped at the palace gate and entered.

Hades asked in surprise: 'Who are you mortals, and what do you want?'

Theseus told him: 'I am Theseus, the bravest king alive.

F

This is my friend Peirithous, who thinks that Queen Persephone is far too good for you. He wants to marry her himself.'

Hades grinned at them. Nobody had ever seen him grin before. 'Well,' he said, 'it is true that Persephone is not exactly happy with me. I might even let her go, if you promise to treat her kindly. Shall we talk the matter over quietly? Please, sit down on that comfortable bench!'

Theseus and Peirithous sat down, but the bench Hades had offered them was a magic one. They became attached to it, so that they could never escape without tearing away part of themselves. Hades stood and roared for laughter, while the Furies whipped the two friends; and ghostly spotted snakes stung them; and Cerberus, waking from his drugged sleep, gnawed at their fingers and toes.

'My poor fools,' chuckled Hades, 'you are here for always!'

SISYPHUS

CHAPTER SEVENTEEN

SISYPHUS

Sisyphus, King of Corinth, who built the Corinthians their first fleet, owned a large herd of cattle. His neighbour Autolycus owned a smaller one.

Autolycus had been kind to Maia, before Hermes's birth —hiding her in his house when the jealous Goddess Hera tried to kill her. So Hermes in gratitude gave Autolycus the magic power of turning bulls into cows, and changing their colours from white to red, or from black to piebald. Autolycus, who was a very clever thief, used to steal Sisyphus's cattle from the pastures next to his own, disguising white bulls as red cows, and black cows as piebald bulls. Sisyphus watched his herd getting smaller, and Autolycus's getting bigger every day. He suspected Autolycus, but could never prove him a thief. At last he hit on the plan of marking the hooves of his remaining cattle with the letters SIS (short for 'Sisyphus'). When more cattle disappeared, Sisyphus sent his soldiers along to Autolycus's cattle yard. They lifted up the hooves of all the cattle there, and found five of them marked 'SIS.'

Autolycus said: 'I never stole them. They are my own cattle. When did Sisyphus have any of this colour? He must have come into my pastures and marked their hooves.'

Everyone argued and shouted. Meanwhile Sisyphus had his revenge. He slipped into Autolycus's house and ran away with his daughter, by whom he became the father of Odysseus, the cleverest of the Greeks who fought at Troy.

One day the River-god Asopus came to Sisyphus, and said: 'You have a bad name for running away with other people's daughters. Have you taken mine?'

'No,' Sisyphus answered. 'But I know where she is.'

'Tell me!'

'First make a spring break out from the hill on which I am building my new city.'

Asopus struck the ground with a magic club and made the spring appear—it was the one beside which Bellerophon caught Pegasus.

Sisyphus then said: 'Zeus has fallen in love with your daughter. They are walking arm in arm in that wooded valley over there.'

Asopus, very angry, went in search of Zeus, who had carelessly left his thunderbolt hanging on a tree. When Asopus ran at him with the club, Zeus escaped and disguised himself as a rock. Asopus rushed past, Zeus turned back again into his true shape, fetched his thunderbolt and threw it at Asopus, who limped ever afterwards from a wounded leg.

Zeus ordered his brother Hades to arrest Sisyphus and give him a really heavy punishment for having betrayed a divine secret to Asopus.

Hades went to Sisyphus. 'Come with me!'

'Certainly not. Hermes is the god who fetches ghosts, not you. Besides, I am not yet due to die. What have you there in that bag?'

'Handcuffs, to keep you from escaping.'

'What are handcuffs?'

'Steel bracelets, chained together. Hephaestus invented them.'

'Show me how they work.'

Hades put on the handcuffs himself. Sisyphus quickly locked them. Then he unchained his dog and fastened the dog's collar around Hades's neck. 'I have you safe now, King Hades,' he laughed.

Though Hades stormed and wept, Sisyphus kept him chained up in the dog's kennel for a whole month. Nobody could die while Hades was a prisoner; and when Ares, God of War, found that battles had become sham fights because nobody got killed, he came to Sisyphus and threatened to strangle him.

'It's no use trying to kill me,' said Sisyphus. 'I have King Hades chained up in my kennel.'

'I know, but I can squeeze your throat until your face turns black and your tongue sticks out. You would hate that. Or I can cut off your head and hide it. Unchain King Hades at once!'

Sisyphus, grumbling, did as Ares ordered. Then he went with him to Tartarus, and told Queen Persephone: 'It is unfair to be taken off like this. I am not even properly buried. King Hades should have left me on the far side of Styx, where the Judges cannot punish me.'

Persephone answered: 'Very well. You may go up again and arrange to be buried with a coin under your tongue, but come back without fail tomorrow.'

Sisyphus went home laughing. When he did not return to Tartarus on the next day, Hades sent Hermes to fetch him.

Sisyphus asked: 'Why? Have the Fates cut off my thread of life?'

Hermes told him: 'Yes. I saw them do it. You should not have given away Zeus's secret to Asopus.'

Sisyphus sighed. 'At any rate, I made him provide a fine spring of water for Corinth.'

'Come, follow me now, and no more tricks, please!'

The rock that the Judges of the Dead ordered Sisyphus to push over the top of the hill in Tartarus was shaped exactly like the one into which Zeus had changed when he hid from Asopus.

But the Corinthians loved Sisyphus because of all he had done for them, and held an annual feast in his honour.

THE LABOURS OF HERACLES

CHAPTER EIGHTEEN

*

THE LABOURS OF HERACLES

Heracles, whom the Romans called Hercules, was Zeus's son by Alcmene, a Theban princess. Hera, angry that Zeus had made another of his marriages with mortal women, sent two tremendous snakes to kill Heracles while still a baby. He and his twin brother Iphicles were lying asleep in a shield, used as a cradle, when the snakes crawled hissing towards them across the floor. Iphicles screamed and rolled out of the shield. But Heracles, an immensely strong child, caught the snakes by their throats, one in each hand, and strangled them.

As a boy, Heracles took far more interest in fighting than in reading, writing, or music; he also preferred roast meat and barley bread to honey cakes and fruit pies. Soon he became the best archer, the best wrestler, and the best boxer alive. Because Linus, his music teacher, beat him for not taking enough trouble over his scales, Heracles knocked Linus dead with a lyre. Accused of murder, Heracles said simply: 'Linus hit me first. All I did was to defend myself.' The judges let him off.

Eurystheus, the High King of Greece, wanted to banish Amphitryon, King of Thebes, now Heracles's stepfather; but Heracles nobly offered to be his slave for ninety-nine months if Amphitryon might stay and keep his throne. Hera advised Eurystheus: 'Agree, but set Heracles the ten most dangerous Labours you can possibly choose, all to be performed in those ninety-nine months. I want him killed.'

The first Labour which Eurystheus set Heracles was to kill the Nemean Lion, an enormous beast, with a skin proof against stone, brass, or iron. It lived in a mountain cave. When the arrows which Heracles shot at the lion bounced off harmlessly, he took his great club of wild-olive wood and hit it on the head; but only smashed the club. The lion shook its head, because of the singing noise in its ears, then yawned and went back to its cave. This cave had two entrances. Heracles netted the smaller with a brass net and, going in by the larger, caught the lion by the throat. Though it bit off the middle finger of his left hand, he managed to get its head under his right arm and squeeze it to death. Heracles skinned the lion by using one of its own claws for a knife, and afterwards wore the skin. Then he cut himself a second club of wild-olive wood and reported to Eurystheus.

The Second Labour was far more dangerous: to kill the monstrous Hydra in the marshes of Lerna. She had a huge body, like a dog's, and eight snake heads on long necks. Heracles fired flaming arrows at the Hydra as she came out from her hole under the roots of a plane tree. Then he rushed forward and battered at the eight heads. As fast as he crushed them, others grew in their places. Up scuttled a crab, sent by Hera, and bit his foot; Heracles broke its shell with a kick. At the same time he drew his sharp, gold-hilted sword and called for Iolaus, his chariot driver. Iolaus hurriedly brought a torch and, after Heracles had cut off each head, singed the neck to prevent a new one from sprouting. That was the end of the Hydra. Heracles dipped his arrows in her poisonous blood. Whoever they struck would die painfully.

The Third Labour was to capture the Ceryneian Hind, a

white deer with brass hooves and golden horns, belonging to the Goddess Artemis. It took Heracles a whole year to catch the hind. He chased her up hill and down dale all over Greece, until at last he shot an unpoisoned arrow at her as she ran past him; the arrow went between the sinew and bone of her forelegs, without drawing a drop of blood, and pinned them together. As she stumbled and fell, Heracles seized her, drew out the arrow, and carried her on his shoulders to Eurystheus. Artemis would have been furious if he had killed her pet hind, but forgave him because she admired his clever shooting. Eurystheus then set the hind free.

The Fourth Labour was to capture the Erymanthian Boar, a huge creature with tusks like an elephant's, and an arrow-proof skin. Heracles chased it to and fro across the mountains in winter, until it stuck in a deep snowdrift. There he jumped in after it and tied its hind legs to its forelegs. When Eurystheus saw Heracles carrying the boar on his back up the palace avenue, he ran off and hid in a big brass jar.

The Fifth Labour was to clean King Augeias's filthy cattle yard in a single day. Augeias owned many thousands of cattle, and never troubled to get rid of the messes they made. Eurystheus set this task just to annoy Heracles, hoping that he would cover himself with filth as he loaded the dung in baskets and carried them away. Augeias stood and sneered at Heracles: 'I bet you twenty cows to one, that you cannot clean the yard in a day.'

'Done,' said Heracles.

He swung his club, knocked down the yard wall, then borrowed a mattock and quickly dug deep channels from two nearby rivers. The river water, rushing through the yard, washed it clean in a very short time.

As his Sixth Labour, Eurystheus told Heracles to free the Stymphalian Marsh of its brass-feathered, man-eating birds. They looked like cranes, but had beaks that would pierce an iron breastplate. Heracles could not swim through the marsh because it was too muddy, nor walk across it because the mud would not bear his weight; and when he shot at the birds his arrows glanced off their feathers.

The Goddess Athene appeared and handed him a brass rattle. 'Shake that!' she ordered. Heracles shook the rattle. The birds rose into the air, mad with terror. He shot and killed scores of them, as they flew off towards the Black Sea; for they had no brass feathers on the undersides of their bodies. None ever returned.

The Seventh Labour was to capture a bull, the terror of Crete. It chased farmers and soldiers, battered down huts and barns, trampled cornfields flat, frightened women and children. This bull had first appeared when Europa's son Minos told the Cretans: 'I am King of this island. Let the gods send me a sign to prove it!' As he spoke, the Cretans saw a snow-white bull with golden horns swimming in from the sea. But instead of sacrificing this beautiful beast to the gods, as he should have done, Minos kept it and sacrificed another. Zeus punished him by letting the bull escape and make trouble all over Crete.

Heracles tracked the bull to a wood. There he climbed a tree, waited for it to pass, and jumped on its back. After a hard struggle he managed to clip a ring through the bull's nose and take it safely across the sea to Eurystheus.

The Eighth Labour was to capture the four savage mares of the Thracian King Diomedes. Diomedes fed these mares on the flesh of strangers who visited his kingdom. Heracles sailed to Thrace, landed near the palace, went straight to Diomedes's stables, chased away the grooms, and drove the

mares plunging and kicking down to the seashore. Alarmed by the noise, Diomedes called the palace guards and hurried in pursuit. Heracles left the mares in charge of his groom Abderus and turned to fight. The battle was short. He stunned Diomedes with his club, and allowed the mares to eat him alive—as they had unfortunately also eaten Abderus, who could not control them. Before he left, Heracles instituted annual funeral games in Abderus's honour. But finding his ship too small for all four mares, he harnessed them to Diomedes's chariot, left the ship behind, and drove home by way of Macedonia.

The Ninth Labour was to get a famous golden girdle from Hippolyte, Queen of the Amazons, who lived on the southern coast of the Black Sea, and bring it back as a present for Eurystheus's daughter. Heracles reached Amazonia without danger. There Queen Hippolyte fell in love with him, and he could have had the girdle as a gift. However, the Goddess Hera spitefully disguised herself as an Amazon and spread the rumour that Heracles had come to kidnap Hippolyte and carry her away to Greece. The angry Amazons jumped on their horses and rode to rescue her, shooting arrows at Heracles as they went. Though Heracles beat off the attack, Hippolyte got killed in the confusion of battle; so he took the girdle from her dead body, and sailed sadly away. He would have liked to marry Hippolyte, and hated giving the girdle to Eurystheus's daughter.

The Tenth Labour was to steal a herd of red cows from King Geryon (who lived on an island near the Ocean Stream). Geryon had three bodies, but only one pair of legs. Hera hoped that Heracles would fail in this last Labour, or else not have time to finish it before the ninety-nine months were up. When he reached the western end of the Mediterranean Sea, where Spain and Africa were joined together in those days, he cut a channel between them; the cliffs on either side are still called 'The Pillars of Heracles'. Then he sailed out into the Ocean in a golden boat lent him by the Sun, using his lion-skin for a sail. As he landed on Geryon's island, a two-headed dog attacked him; he struck it dead with a swing of his club, and did the same to Geryon's herdsman. Lastly, Geryon himself rushed from his palace, like a row of three men. The Goddess Hera tried to help him by flashing a mirror in Heracles's eyes, but he dodged and killed Geryon with an arrow shot sideways through all his three bodies. Then he shot at Hera, too, wounding her in the shoulder. She flew off, screaming for Apollo and Artemis to draw out the arrow and make her well again.

Heracles drove the red cows across the Pyrenees and along the south coast of France. At the Alps, however, a messenger of Hera's misdirected him, on purpose. He turned right and went all the way down to the Straits of Messina before he realized that this was Italy, not Greece. Angrily he turned back, and wasted still more time when he reached what is now Trieste, because Hera sent her gadfly, which stung the cows in their tenderest parts. They stampeded eastward, and Heracles had to follow their tracks for five or six hundred miles, as far as the Crimea. There an ugly, snaked-tailed woman promised to round them up, on condition that he kissed her three times. He did so, though grudging every kiss, and at last came safely home to Greece with the cows, just as the ninety-nine months ended.

Heracles should now have been set free but, on Hera's advice, Eurystheus said: 'You did not perform my Second Labour properly, because you called in your friend Iolaus to help kill the Hydra. And you did not perform my Fifth Labour properly either, because Augeias paid you for cleaning his cattle yard.'

'How unfair!' cried Heracles. 'I called Iolaus because Hera interfered: she sent a crab to bite my foot. And though Augeias certainly betted me twenty cows to one that I could not clean the cattle yard in a day, I would have performed the Labour anyhow.'

'No argument, please! You made the bet; so instead of working for me alone, you got twenty cows from another man.'

'Nonsense! Augeias refused to pay me. He claimed that I had not cleaned the yard myself—the River-god did it.'

'He was quite right. The Labour should not count as your own work. You must perform two more, but you may take your time over them.'

'Agreed,' said Heracles, 'and if I live to complete them, it will be the worse for your family.'

Eurystheus had thought of two very dangerous extra Labours. The first was to fetch the Golden Apples of the Hesperides from the Far West. These apples were the fruit of a tree once given by Mother Earth to Hera as a wedding present. The Hesperides, the Titan Atlas's daughters, tended the tree; and Ladon, an unsleeping dragon, coiled around it.

Heracles visited the Caucasus to ask Prometheus's advice. Prometheus welcomed him, saying: 'Please, drive off that vulture. It prevents me from thinking clearly.' Heracles not only drove away the vulture, but shot it dead and begged Zeus to forgive Prometheus. Zeus, who felt that the punishment had lasted quite long enough, kindly allowed Heracles to break the chains. However, he ordered Prometheus always to wear an iron finger ring, as a reminder of his slavery. This was how rings first came into fashion.

Prometheus now warned Heracles not to pick the apples himself, because any mortal who did so would drop dead at once. 'Persuade some immortal to pick them for you,' he suggested. After a farewell feast, Heracles sailed towards Morocco. On reaching Tangier, he walked inland to where Atlas, the rebellious Titan, was holding up the Heavens. Heracles asked: 'If I take on your duty for an hour, will you be willing to pick me three apples from your daughters' tree?'

'Certainly,' said Atlas, 'if you first kill the unsleeping dragon.'

Heracles drew his bow and shot Ladon over the garden wall. Then he stood behind Atlas and, straddling his legs wide apart, took the weight of the Heavens on his own head and shoulders. Atlas climbed the wall, greeted his daughters, stole the apples, and shouted to Heracles: 'Be good enough to stay there just a little longer, while I carry these apples to Eurystheus. With my huge legs I should be back here in an hour's time.'

Though Heracles knew that Atlas would never deliver the apples, but go off to rescue the other Titans instead, and start a new rebellion, he pretended to trust him. 'With pleasure,' he answered, 'if you will please take the weight from me again for one moment more, while I fold up this lion-skin to make a comfortable head pad.'

Atlas laid down the apples and did as Heracles asked. Heracles then took the apples and walked away. 'You tried to trick me,' he said, laughing, 'but I have tricked you. Goodbye!'

As Heracles went home through Libya, a gigantic son of Mother Earth, by name Antaeus, challenged him to a wrestling match. Heracles oiled himself all over, so that Antaeus could not get a firm grip of him; Antaeus, on the contrary, rubbed himself with sand. Every time Heracles threw Antaeus hard to the ground, he was surprised to see him rise again stronger than ever because touching Mother

G

Earth renewed his strength. Realizing what he must do, Heracles lifted Antaeus off the ground, cracked his ribs, and held him aloft out of Mother Earth's reach, until he died. A month later Heracles brought the apples safely to Eurystheus.

The last and worst Labour was to capture the dog Cerberus, and drag him up from Tartarus. On receiving this order, Heracles went for purification to Eleusis, where Demeter's Mysteries were held, and now cleansed of all defilement boldly descended to Tartarus. Charon refused to ferry a live mortal across the Styx.

'I will wreck your boat,' Heracles threatened, 'and fill you as full of arrows as a hedgehog is full of prickles.'

Charon shivered in terror and ferried him across. Hades afterwards punished Charon for his cowardice.

Heracles saw Theseus and Peirithous stuck to Hades's bench, and being whipped by the Furies. He gave Theseus an enormous tug and wrenched him free, though a large part of his back stayed behind. But finding it impossible to release Peirithous, except with an axe, he left him there.

Persephone darted from the palace and took Heracles by both hands. 'Can I help you, dear Heracles?' she asked.

'Be kind enough to lend me your watchdog for a few days, Your Majesty. He can run home again as soon as I have shown him to Eurystheus.'

Persephone turned to King Hades: 'Please, Husband, grant Heracles what he asks. This is a task set him on your sister-in-law Hera's advice. He promises not to keep our dog Cerberus.'

Hades answered: 'Very well, and he may take that fool Theseus back, too, while he is about it. Still, I must make it a rule that he masters Cerberus without the use of club or arrows.'

Hades thought this a safe condition, but Heracles's lion-skin was proof against the blows of Cerberus's barbed tail; and his strong hands squeezed Cerberus's throat until all three heads turned black. Cerberus fainted, and let himself be dragged up on earth. Unfortunately, the only tunnel wide enough for him was one that came out near Mariandyne, beside the Black Sea; so Heracles had a long and difficult journey. Before starting, he took a branch of the white poplar with him for a trophy, and wore it as a wreath.

Eurystheus was nearly scared to death when Heracles appeared, dragging Cerberus behind him on a leash. 'Thank you, noble Heracles,' he said, 'you are now free of your Labours. But please send that brute back at once.'

Heracles returned to Thebes, where his mother Alcmena welcomed him joyfully. Then Hera thought of a clever plot. She told Autolycus to steal a heard of dappled mares and foals from a man named Iphitus, change their colour, and sell them to Heracles. Iphitus tracked the herd all the way to Tiryns by their hoofprints, and asked Heracles whether he had taken them by any chance. Heracles led Iphitus to the top of a high tower, and said grimly: 'Look around you! Can you see any dappled mares in my pastures?'

'No,' answered Iphitus. 'But I know that they are somewhere about.'

Heracles, losing his temper at being thought a thief and a liar, flung Iphitus over the battlements.

The gods sentenced Heracles to be the slave of Queen Omphale of Lydia; the money he fetched at his sale, which Hermes had arranged, went to Iphitus's orphan children. Omphale, who did not know who Heracles was, asked him what he could do. 'Anything you like, madam,' he answered readily. So she made him dress as a woman, in a yellow petticoat, handed him a distaff, and showed him how to spin wool. Heracles found the work very restful. One day a gigantic dragon started eating Omphale's Lydian subjects, and she said to Heracles: 'You look a strong man. Dare you fight the dragon?'

'At your service, madam.'

Dragons were nothing to Heracles. He shot a poisoned arrow between this dragon's jaws, and Omphale gratefully gave him his freedom.

Later, Heracles married a princess named Deianeira, a daughter of the God Dionysus, and founded the Olympic Games, which were to be held every four years as long as the world should last. He ruled that the winners of each event were to be given wreaths, instead of the usual valuable prizes, because he had not been paid for his Labours either. No man dared wrestle against Heracles, which disappointed the spectators. However, King Zeus kindly came down from Olympus. He and Heracles had a wonderful tussle together. The match ended in a draw, and everyone cheered.

Heracles now took vengeance on kings who had treated him scornfully while he was performing his Labours, including Augeias, and killed three of Eurystheus's sons. Zeus forbade him to attack Eurystheus himself. That would set a bad example to other freed slaves. The River-god Achelous challenged Heracles to a fight, but lost a horn in the struggle. Heracles also fought the God Ares and sent him hobbling back to Olympus.

One day a Centaur named Nessus offered to carry Heracles's wife, Deianeira, across a flooded river for a small fee. Heracles paid the money, but Nessus, having reached the farther bank, galloped off with Deianeira in his arms. Heracles shot Nessus, at a distance of half a mile, using one of the arrows dipped in the Hydra's blood. The dying Nessus whispered to Deianeira: 'Collect a little of my blood in this small oil jar. Then, if Heracles ever loves another woman more than you, here is a sure charm to use. The oil will keep my blood from drying up. Spread it on his shirt. He will never be unfaithful again. Goodbye!' Deianeira did as Nessus advised.

While still serving Eurystheus, Heracles had taken part in an archery contest proposed by King Eurytus of Oechalia, the prize of which was his daughter Iole. Eurytus boasted himself the best archer in Greece, and felt very cross at being beaten by Heracles. He shouted: 'My daughter is a princess. I cannot possibly marry her to Eurystheus's slave. The competition is void.' Remembering this insult some years later, Heracles sacked Oechalia, killed Eurytus, and took away Iole, with her two sisters, to scrub floors and cook. Deianeira feared that he might fall in love with Iole, who was very beautiful. When he sent a messenger home, asking Deianeira for his best embroidered shirt, she thought: 'He wants to wear it when he marries Iole.' So she smeared some of Nessus's blood on the red embroidery of the shirt, where it would not show, and handed it to the messenger.

Heracles really needed the shirt for a thanksgiving sacrifice to Zeus, after the capture of Oechalia. He put it on, and was pouring wine on the altar when he suddenly felt as though he were being bitten by scorpions. The heat of his body had melted the Hydra's poison in Nessus's blood. He yelled, bellowed, shrieked, knocked over the altar, and tried to rip off the shirt; but great lumps of flesh came away too. His blood hissed with the poison. Then he jumped into a stream; the poison burned him worse than before. Heracles knew that he was doomed.

He begged his friends in an unsteady voice: 'Please, carry me to Mount Oeta, and build a pyre of oak and wild-olive.' They obeyed, weeping. Heracles climbed to the platform at the top, and calmly lay down on his lion-skin, using his club for a pillow. He let himself be burned to death; the fire hurt far less than the Hydra's poison.

Zeus felt proud of his brave son. He told the Olympians: 'Heracles will be our porter, and marry my daughter Hebe, the Goddess of Youth. If anyone objects, I shall start throwing thunderbolts. Rise, noble soul of Heracles! Welcome to Olympus!'

Zeus looked so fierce that Hera dared say nothing. Heracles's immortal soul ascended on a cloud, and Athene was soon introducing him to the other gods. Only Ares turned his back, but when Demeter begged him not to be a fool he too shook hands with Heracles—rather rudely.

Deianeira, hearing that she had caused Heracles's death, took a sword and stabbed herself.

THE GIANTS' REBELLION

CHAPTER NINETEEN

THE GIANTS' REBELLION

When Antaeus was killed, Mother Earth complained to the Olympians. She said that, to make amends, Zeus should at least pardon Atlas and the other Titans, her sons, who were still held in perpetual slavery. Zeus gruffly told her to be silent. In revenge, Mother Earth visited Phlegra in Thrace, and there created twenty-four enormous giants with long beards and snakes' tails for feet. They planned to attack the Olympians, throwing rocks and firebrands up at the palace. Hera prophesied that the Olympians' only hope lay in finding a flower which grew somewhere on earth; whoever smelt it would never be wounded. So Zeus ordered the Sun and Moon not to shine for awhile, then groped all about Greece until he found the flower and made all the Olympians sniff at it. Hera prophesied again: 'Now a champion in a lion-skin will save us.' This, of course, meant Heracles, their new porter.

The gods marched out of Olympus and invaded Phlegra. Heracles fitted an arrow to his bow and shot Alcyoneus, the leader of the Giants, who fell down as if dead, but sprang up at once, revived by touching his native soil. Heracles wrestled with Alcyoneus, dragged him over the Greek frontier into Scythia, and there clubbed him to death. Meanwhile, the other Giants made a charge, drove the Olympians back up Mount Olympus, and heaped an enormous pile of

105

rocks outside the steep walls from which to jump across into the palace. A stone struck Ares on the head. He dropped to his knees, groaning. A Giant named Porphyrion tried to strangle Hera, but Eros shot him in the heart with his little bow, so that he fell madly in love, seized her hand and gave it great slobbering kisses. Zeus, very angry, threw a thunderbolt at Porphyrion, who caught it on his shield and kissed Hera again full on the mouth. Heracles returned just in time to break the Giant's neck and hold him aloft until he died. To help Ares, Apollo shot out a Giant's right eye, while Heracles shot out the left. Hephaestus blinded another Giant with a ladleful of molten gold thrown in his face. Then Heracles picked up both Giants, and hurried them across the frontier, one under each arm, and knocked them on the head. While the battle raged, Aphrodite hid in a linen closet. Demeter and Hestia stood shivering at one of the palace windows. But Athene fought coolly and well, and Artemis darted about shooting Giants in the most awkward places. Aroused by the noise, the Three Fates left their spinning room and ran to the kitchen, where each armed herself with a golden pestle of the kind used to pound parsley or mint or garlic in a mortar. All the Giants fled, for nobody can fight against the Fates.

The Olympians threw at the retreating enemy whatever came to hand. One enormous rock hurled by Poseidon fell into the sea and became the island of Nisyrus. The Giants made their last stand at Trapezus in Arcadia. Poseidon, Zeus, and Ares, who had not done very well so far, now fought fiercely with thunderbolts, trident, and spear; while Hermes, who had borrowed Hades's helmet of invisibility, stabbed the enemy from behind. Heracles, however, killed more Giants than all the other gods together. As soon as the battle was over, Hera came up and thanked him for getting rid of that disgusting Porphyrion. She said: 'I am ashamed to think how badly I treated you on earth.'

'Please forget about it, Queen Hera,' Heracles answered, and made her a low bow.

TWO OTHER REBELLIONS

CHAPTER TWENTY

*

TWO OTHER REBELLIONS

On the advice of Mother Earth, the twin Aloeids—gigantic mortals who grew six feet taller and two feet broader every year—decided to steal the food of immortality, banish the Olympians, and rule the world themselves. First they caught Ares at his country house in Thrace and, after binding his arms and legs, locked him in a brass chest. Then they took the huge mountain of Pelion and piled it on its neighbour, Mount Ossa, so that now they could throw rocks on Olympus from above.

'I shall marry Queen Hera,' boasted the elder, whose name was Ephialtes.

'And I shall marry Artemis,' boasted Otus, the younger.

Apollo drew his sister aside. 'Artemis, you alone can save us.'

'How?'

'By promising to marry Otus.'

'Brother, I would rather die than marry!'

'You need not keep the promise. Use your common sense. You can easily send both twins down to Tartarus and be rid of them.'

'Surely not? Hera has prophesied that no gods and no other mortals can kill them.'

'Maybe. But there is a catch to every prophecy.'

So Artemis promised to meet Otus on the island of Naxos,

and marry him there. Ephialtes grew very jealous when Hermes brought Otus her message. He growled: 'Why has Hera not promised to come too? Surely she prefers me to Zeus? I am by far the stronger.'

Otus laughed: 'You may be strong, but how do you expect a goddess to fall in love with your ugly face?'

'What about yours?'

'Artemis admires it.'

'Does she? Well, in that case she can admire mine. I am the elder of us two, and when she arrives I shall marry her, not Hera!'

'No, Artemis is for me. Besides, she knows that I am a far better archer than you.'

'Liar! Prove it!'

As they stood quarrelling, Artemis disguised herself as one of her own white hinds, and rushed between them. The giants seized their bows. Otus shot at her from the left, and Ephialtes from the right. She went so fast that both missed; and then both fell dead—each with an arrow through his head. No gods could kill them, and no other mortals; but they had killed themselves.

Hermes conducted the Aloeids to Tartarus for punishment, and then rescued Ares, half dead, from the brass chest.

Mother Earth made one last attempt to get rid of the Olympians. She created Typhon, the hugest monster ever seen. He had an ass's head, with ears that touched the stars, wings that blacked out the sky, and a mass of coiled snakes instead of legs. Typhon so terrified the Olympians by rushing towards the palace, spouting flame, that they fled to Egypt. Zeus went disguised as a ram; Hera as a cow; Apollo as a crow; Poseidon as a horse; Artemis as a wildcat; Ares as a boar; Hermes as a crane; and so forth. Only Athene refused to stir: she called Zeus a coward, and said that she was ashamed to acknowledge herself his daughter.

Zeus blushed, turned back into his proper shape, and flung a thunderbolt at Typhon, wounding him in the shoulder. With a yell of pain, Typhon seized Zeus, beat him black and blue, then pulled out the sinews from his feet and hands to make him helpless, and left him in charge of a she-monster named Delphyne.

Typhon asked the Fates for medicine, because his shoulder was hurting. Silently they handed him some apples, and went on spinning. He crunched the fruit in his huge teeth, but the Fates had tricked him by giving him death-apples. Typhon grew weaker and weaker as the poison took effect.

Hermes, Apollo, and Pan visited Delphyne's cave by night. Pan raised a sudden horrible shout, which made Delphyne jump nearly out of her skin. Hermes slipped in unnoticed, stole the sinews from a chest under her bed, and fixed them to Zeus's feet and hands. Apollo then shot Delphyne dead, and Zeus pelted the feeble Typhon with thunderbolts, finally hurling an enormous rock on top of him. The rock is now Mount Etna in Sicily. From time to time, Typhon's fiery breath rushes up through the crater, blowing forth smoke, lava, and pumice stone.

JASON AND THE GOLDEN FLEECE

CHAPTER TWENTY-ONE

*

JASON AND THE GOLDEN FLEECE

Queen Ino, hating her stepson Phrixus, plotted against his life. She persuaded the women of Boeotia, the country in which she and Phrixus's father, King Athamas, lived, to bake all the barley seed secretly in ovens, so that when it was sown in the spring not a single seed would come up. Knowing that Athamas would then send messengers to ask the Delphic Oracle whether the Olympians were angry with him, she had bribed the messengers to bring back a lie: 'The Oracle says that unless Athamas sacrifices his son Phrixus on a mountain-top, no barley will ever grow in Boeotia.'

Athamas felt that he must obey. He took Phrixus to the top of a mountain near Thebes and would have sacrificed him there to Zeus if Heracles had not happened to be passing by on his way home from capturing King Diomedes's mares. 'Zeus loathes human sacrifices,' Heracles shouted, knocking the knife out of Athamas's hand.

'But I must obey the Delphic Oracle,' said Athamas, weeping.

At that moment Zeus sent a winged golden ram flying down from Olympus. Phrixus climbed on its back. His little sister Helle, who loved him, pleaded: 'Take me too, or else Father will kill me instead of you!' Phrixus pulled her up behind him, and the ram headed east to the land of Colchis, at the other end of the Black Sea. Helle, feeling air-sick, fell

H

off halfway, and drowned in the strait afterwards called 'The Hellespont'.

Phrixus flew on. When he reached Colchis, he sacrificed the ram to Zeus and hung its golden fleece in a temple of Ares, where a huge serpent guarded it. Phrixus lived for several years longer and married a Colchian princess, by whom he had four sons. But in Colchis men were not properly buried—their bodies were always wrapped in oxhide, tied to the top of trees, and then eaten by vultures. Phrixus's ghost returned and complained to his friend, King Pelias, who had recently seized the throne of Iolcus in Thessaly, that he could not gain admittance to Tartarus.

Pelias, because the Delphic Oracle had prophesied that a young relation would kill him, invited all his cousins and nephews to a banquet and massacred them. That very evening, however, a new nephew named Jason was born, and Jason's mother told her maids to weep over the baby as though it had died at birth. Later, Pelias killed the mother to prevent her having any more children; but Jason had been safely smuggled away to Mount Pelion, where Cheiron the wise Centaur educated him in secret. The oracle then warned Pelias: 'Beware of a one-sandalled man!'

Twenty years passed. As Pelias, now very old, was sacrificing on the seashore of Iolcus, he saw a stranger approaching, armed with two broad-bladed spears, and wearing only one sandal. 'Who are you?' he asked.

'I am your nephew Jason.'

'Why are you not wearing two sandals?'

'I lost the other in the river as I carried an old woman across. She turned out to be the Goddess Hera in disguise and blamed you for never sacrificing to her.'

Pelias glared at Jason. 'What would you do if an oracle prophesied that one of your own relations would kill you?'

Hera disguised herself as a fly, and whispered some words in Jason's ear. He repeated after her: 'I should make him go to Colchis, bury the bones of Phrixus there, and bring back the Golden Fleece.'

Pelias said: 'You must be the man I was warned against. Go off at once and bring me that fleece!'

Jason sent heralds to every part of Greece, inviting heroes to join him in the adventure; and soon hundreds arrived at Iolcus. He was obliged to refuse most of them because the *Argo*, the ship now being built for him, would seat only fifty rowers. When Heracles, who had just captured the Erymanthian Boar, joined the crew, everyone wanted him to command the expedition. He answered: 'No, that must be Jason's honour, not mine. I am still a slave.'

The Argonauts, as the crew of heroes were called, sailed eastward from Iolcus in early spring, and presently put in at the island of Lemnos for food and water. A few months before, the Lemnian women had murdered all their husbands, for treating them in a cruel way, but were now feeling lost and lonely. These women tried to make the Argonauts stay, and marry them. Heracles fetched everyone aboard again by main force.

The *Argo* sailed up the Hellespont, past Troy, and into the Sea of Marmara. There the Argonauts had a friendly competition as to which of them could row the longest. Heracles, Jason, and the Heavenly Twins (Castor and Polydeuces) held out one entire night and until breakfast-time the next day. By mid-day only Jason and Heracles were left —one rowing on each side of the ship. Towards evening Jason fainted, and Heracles's oar snapped at the same moment; so they beached the *Argo* on the coast of Mysia, and prepared supper—all except Heracles, who went to cut a new oar. He had an orphan with him, named Hylas, now

115

acting as cabin-boy. While the Argonauts shot and cut up some deer, Hylas took his pitcher to fill with water for the stew. He was never seen again. Heracles ran to and fro shouting: 'Hylas! Hylas!' at the top of his voice, not knowing that a Naiad who lived in the pool from which Hylas filled his pitcher had fallen in love with the pretty boy and pulled him under the water. Heracles wanted the Argonauts to declare war on the Mysian peasants, whom he accused of stealing Hylas. He got so excited and behaved so strangely— they saw, for example, that his new oar was twice the size of all the others—that they sailed away next night, and left him behind.

Near the place where Constantinople afterwards stood they found Cadmus's brother, King Phineus, in a very unhappy state. As soon as his servants laid a meal for him, three disgusting birds with women's faces and foul breaths, called Harpies, used to swoop down on the table. Whatever food they could not carry off, they breathed on and made quite uneatable. The Argonauts chased away the Harpies, and Phineus gratefully gave Jason good advice. His last words were: 'And when you reach Colchis, trust in the Goddess Aphrodite!'

To enter the Black Sea, the *Argo* must first pass through the Bosphorus strait. These were guarded by two floating rocks which clashed together and crushed any ship as it tried to enter. Phineus had advised the Argonauts to take a dove with them. On reaching the Clashing Rocks, Jason released the dove. Though it shot ahead, the rocks nipped its tail feathers. The *Argo* followed at full speed behind. The rocks quickly opened and closed again, nipping off her stern ornament. Zeus then anchored them fast forever. Since the current in the strait ran very strongly, Orpheus, who was one of the Argonauts, twanged his lyre and the rowers kept

time to the music; they entered the Black Sea after a great struggle.

Halfway along the southern coast, the *Argo* reached the island of Ares, where the brass-feathered birds, driven from the Stymphalian Marshes by Heracles, had now settled. The Argonauts sailed quickly past, clashing their brass shields with swords to frighten the birds off. On the next day, they rescued a party of shipwrecked travellers. These turned out to be the four sons of Phrixus, who were making a voyage to Greece, in the hope that King Athamas might name them as his heirs. Jason warned them to expect nothing from Athamas, now banished to a desert place in Thessaly, and invited them to join his Argonauts. There would be room for them aboard, because he had lost Heracles and three other members of the crew in various accidents. Phrixus's sons accepted the invitation and swore to obey Jason's orders. Jason called a council of war in a backwater of the River Phasis, and sacrificed to Aphrodite. The goddess appeared and promised him help. She found her naughty son Eros rolling dice against Zeus's cup-bearer Ganymede, and bribed him with a beautiful golden ball, enamelled in blue, to do as she told him. Eros took off for the palace of King Aeëtes at Colchis, hid behind a pillar, and got ready to shoot the King's youngest daughter, Medea. Jason came up soon afterwards, guided by Phrixus's sons, and asked King Aeëtes politely whether he might have the Golden Fleece as a favour.

'I will conquer all your enemies if you give it to me,' he said.

Aeëtes refused. 'Go home, young man, before I cut out your tongue!'

But Medea pleaded: 'Father, do remember your manners! This brave prince has saved the lives of your four grandchildren.'

118

Eros let fly his arrow, and Medea at once fell madly in love with Jason. She begged Aeëtes to give him the Fleece on condition that he perform certain tasks.

Aeëtes agreed crossly. 'But they are going to be extremely difficult tasks,' he told Jason. 'I have two fire-breathing bulls. Yoke them, plough a four-acre field, and sow it with dragon's teeth. Here is a bagful of them, which Cadmus did not use.'

Having made Jason swear by all the gods to be her husband so long as he lived, Medea helped him by smearing the juice of a certain Colchian crocus on his body. This juice protected him against the bulls' fiery breaths. He yoked the bulls, ploughed the field, sowed the teeth and, when armed men sprang up, did exactly what Cadmus had done—threw a stone in their midst and so provoked them to kill one another.

In the meantime, Phrixus's four sons, at Jason's orders, took down their father's bones from the tree on which they were still hanging in an oxhide, buried them with a silver coin for Charon, and raised a neat headstone over them.

When Aeëtes found that Jason had completed the tasks, he shouted: 'You shall not have the Fleece, rascal! My daughter helped you unfairly. And why did you bury Phrixus's bones? Burial is forbidden in our laws. You must leave Colchis before dawn.'

That night, Medea led Jason to the temple where the Fleece hung from a pillar and sang magic spells to the serpent, sprinkling poppy juice on its eyes until they closed in sleep. Then Jason stole the Fleece and ran with her to the *Argo*. After a fierce fight the Argonauts beat off the Colchian army, and rowed away down the river. Medea healed their wounds with ointment from her medicine box.

Aeëtes's fleet pursued the *Argo* through the Black Sea, the strait of Bosphorus, the Sea of Marmara, the Aegean Sea, and all around Greece, as far as the island of Drepane (now called Corfu), halfway up the Adriatic Sea. Medea and Jason had landed there at mid-day, and asked the King and Queen for protection. The Admiral of the Colchian Fleet visited the palace at supper-time, and said: 'Your Majesty, a rascal named Jason has run off with King Aeëtes's daughter, the Princess Medea. We are sent to fetch her home, and also the Golden Fleece, which they have stolen.'

The King answered: 'It is too late in the day for me to decide whether you have a right to take away either Medea or the Fleece. Return in the morning, when my head is clearer.'

The Goddess Aphrodite appeared to the Queen, saying: 'Let me lend you my golden girdle, to make the King fall in love with you all over again and do everything you ask.'

'That would be delightful. He has been getting rather tired of me lately. But what shall I ask him?'

'Ask him to send the Colchians home.'

When the Queen buckled on the girdle, the King exclaimed: 'Darling, how utterly beautiful you are! Can I do anything for you?'

'I want a new crown, with diamonds and rubies and emeralds; and a long, embroidered gold cloak. Also, I want to know what you are going to tell the Colchian Admiral tomorrow.'

'I promise you the crown and the cloak. But I have not yet decided what I shall say tomorrow.'

'Well, allow me to advise you. Tell the Admiral that if Princess Medea has not yet married Jason, she must go home to her father King Aeëtes with the Fleece. But if she *has* already married him, then Jason may keep her, and count the Fleece as his wedding present.'

'All right, I will say that—if you let me give you a hundred kisses!'

She counted the kisses carefully, gave him one extra, and then went to Jason—first taking off the girdle, for fear he might fall in love with her too and make Medea jealous. 'Hurry,' she cried, 'and get married at once!'

The Argonauts arranged a midnight wedding for Jason and Medea. Next morning, the King heard what had happened and told the Admiral that Medea and the Fleece were both Jason's now.

The Admiral dared not fight the Argonauts; but neither did he dare go back empty-handed. He asked the King's leave to settle in Drepane with his whole fleet. This was granted him. Some months later, the news reached King Aeëtes at Colchis. He died of rage.

The Argonauts, sailing home to Iolcus, were caught by a violent wind and blown towards the coast of Africa. There, an enormous wave picked up the *Argo* and left her high and dry on the desert sands. They would have been forced to abandon her, if the Goddess Libya had not appeared, dressed in goatskins, and lent them wooden rollers. The Argonauts then pushed the *Argo* into the water again.

They sailed to Crete, where a bronze mechanical man, made in Hephaestus's smithy, guarded the harbours by hurling rocks at foreign ships. Since they needed food and water, Medea bewitched the bronze man with her eyes. He staggered about, struck his heel against a rock, and bled to death. The Argonauts went safely ashore.

They reached Iolcus without further adventure early one October evening. A single fisherman sat on the beach mending his nets. When he told the Argonauts that Pelias had given orders for Jason to be murdered at sight, Medea disguised herself as an aged woman and took her Colchian maids along to the palace. There she pretended to be a goddess come from Britain in a fiery chariot. 'I shall make you young again, King Pelias,' she told him.

Pelias watched Medea cut up an old ram and boil the pieces in an iron pot, using magic herbs and spells. Then she did a conjuring trick: she pulled a year-old lamb from the pot, saying: 'This is the ram which I cut up. Look at him now! The same spells will work for you.'

'If you can make old people young, why not be young yourself?' Pelias asked cautiously.

'I will, if it amuses you. Shut your eyes, and count to a hundred!'

While Pelias counted, she quickly took off her disguise. 'Open your eyes!'

Seeing Medea suddenly become young and beautiful, Pelias told one of his daughters to chop him up with an axe and boil his pieces in the pot. This daughter, it turned out, was the young relation fated to kill him, because the pot, of course, contained no real magic.

Jason hung up the Golden Fleece in a temple of Zeus, on the mountain near Thebes from which the ram had carried off Phrixus. Then he sailed the *Argo* to Corinth, beached her, and offered her as a gift to the God Poseidon.

Corinthus, the King of Corinth, died suddenly. Jason was chosen to take his place. But the townspeople found that Corinthus had died of poison, and Medea confessed to the crime. So they asked Jason to marry someone else, and remain King. He agreed, on condition that they would spare Medea's life.

Medea said: 'You swore by all the gods to be my husband for life.'

'I did not know that you were a poisoner,' Jason answered. 'You had better go away quickly, before the Corinthians change their minds about punishing you. I am marrying the Princess Glauce.'

A golden crown and a long white gown were sent to

Glauce. The messenger who brought them said: 'Wedding gifts from Hera.' They really came from Medea. As soon as Glauce put them on, they burst into flames, and burned her to death. The palace caught fire, and the guests were trapped by the flames. Only Jason escaped.

Medea fled, and later married King Aegeus of Athens, as has already been told. The Olympians cursed Jason for breaking faith with Medea. He lost his throne, and wandered miserably all over Greece, avoided by his former friends. In old age, he went back to Corinth, dressed like a beggar, and sat in the shade of the *Argo*, weeping to think of his past glories. The prow fell and killed him. But Zeus set the stern in the Heavens, as the constellation *Argo*.

ALCESTIS

CHAPTER TWENTY-TWO

*

ALCESTIS

Several kings wanted to marry Alcestis, the most beautiful of King Pelias's daughters. Not long before the *Argo* returned to Iolcus, Pelias announced that he would give her in marriage to whatever king could harness a wild boar and a lion to his chariot, and drive it around the local race course. Many kings tried and failed.

But King Admetus of Pherae sent for the God Apollo, who was then serving him as a slave, in punishment for having murdered the Cyclopes.

'Have you been well treated here, Apollo?' Admetus asked.

'Very well indeed, Your Majesty. Some mortal kings would have set me disgusting tasks, just to show how important they were. But you have been more like a friend than a master.'

'In that case, please do me a particular favour!'

'By all means.'

'Come to Iolcus, and help me yoke a wild boar and a lion to my chariot.'

'At your orders!'

Apollo brought his lyre to Iolcus. He played so sweetly that the wild boar stood still with its mouth open; and the lion began purring like a cat. Admetus found it easy to harness and drive them.

Next day, Admetus married Alcestis, but by mistake did not offer Apollo's sister Artemis the usual sacrifice; so she turned Alcestis into a long wriggling snake. Admetus again sent for Apollo, who comforted him: 'Do not weep, Your Majesty. I shall tell my sister that you have been a good master, and never meant to insult her.'

At Apollo's wish, Artemis turned Alcestis back into a woman. 'Thank you, dear Sister!' said Apollo. 'Now, while you are about it, will you do me one more favour? Arrange with Hades that when Admetus's last day arrives, some other member of his family may go down to Tartarus instead of him.'

Artemis asked Hades whether it mattered much whose ghost he got, so long as it arrived punctually.

'No,' answered Hades, 'but it must come willingly as well as punctually.'

Then one day Hermes entered Admetus's bedroom. 'Follow me, please, to Tartarus!'

'Apollo! Apollo! Help!' cried Admetus.

Apollo appeared, and shook Hermes by the hand. 'Wait a minute, brother! King Hades has promised Artemis that someone else may die for Admetus.'

'Admetus must hurry. The Fates are about to snip the thread of his life.'

'I will delay them. Hurry, Admetus: find a substitute!'

Apollo flew to Olympus, begged a huge cup of wine from Dionysus, and took it to the spinning room. 'Taste this!' he told the Fates. They tasted the wine, and smacked their withered lips. The eldest one, Atropos, laid down her shears and cried: 'Give me another cup!' She drank so much that Admetus gained three or four hours.

First he went to his parents, who were nearly a hundred

127

years old. 'Will either of you die for me?' he asked them.

'Certainly not! What an unkind son you are! We have just begun to enjoy life.'

Admetus went to two wretched prisoners in the dungeon, who had been begging him to put them out of their misery. He asked: 'Will either of you die for me?'

'Certainly not! The sooner you die, the happier we shall be. Perhaps the next king will release us.'

Admetus went to a poor man suffering from an incurable disease, and asked him: 'Will you die for me?'

'Certainly not! People call my disease incurable, but there is always hope: Asclepius might come along and save me.'

At that moment Alcestis arrived back from Iolcus, where she had been the only one of King Pelias's three daughters not to be deceived by Medea's pretence of making him young again. 'I refuse to cut up my father,' she had said, 'even if he orders it. I am going straight home.'

She was met at the palace gate by Admetus. 'Nobody will die for me,' he whined. 'I suppose it is useless to ask even you, who pretend to love me best?'

Alcestis kissed her two young sons goodbye. Then she swallowed a deadly poison and beckoned to Hermes. 'Take me with you!' she said firmly.

Yet that was not the end.

When Alcestis reached Tartarus, Persephone came out of the palace to meet her. 'Go home at once, madam! I cannot allow beautiful women to die for their selfish husbands.'

'But King Hades will not let me go, now that I am here.'

'Leave me to manage him. *I* know how husbands should be treated. Off with you at once, by the side stairs!'

Alcestis returned to the children, who ran and hugged her. After a violent quarrel with Persephone, Hades knocked at Admetus's gate. He had come to fetch Alcestis back.

But Apollo called Heracles down from Olympus to protect her.

'Had you not better obey Hades's orders, darling?' asked Admetus nervously.

'You stay here, Queen Alcestis!' growled Heracles.

On Apollo's advice, Admetus then sacrificed a pig to Hades. 'The pig's soul can take my place,' he muttered in a shaky voice.

Hades disliked the exchange, but Heracles's olive-wood club frightened him. He went off, grumbling. 'Very well: I accept the pig's soul. Yours is not worth much more than that, you coward! Fancy expecting your poor parents to die for you!'

'What ever made you drink poison?' Heracles asked Alcestis.

'I did it for my children's sake. If Admetus had died, their uncle would have seized the throne and murdered them.'

'*That* explains everything,' said Heracles.

PERSEUS

CHAPTER TWENTY-THREE

*

PERSEUS

An oracle had warned Acrisius, King of Argos, that his grandson would kill him. 'Then I shall take care to have no grandchildren,' Acrisius grunted. Going home, he locked Danaë, his only daughter, in a tower with brass doors, guarded by a savage dog, and brought all her food with his own hands.

Zeus fell in love with Danaë when he saw her, from far off, leaning sadly over the battlements. To disguise himself from Hera, Zeus became a shower of golden rain and descended on the tower. Danaë hurried downstairs, the rain trickled after her, and then Zeus changed back into his own shape. 'Will you marry me?' he asked Danaë.

'Yes,' she answered, 'I am very lonely here.'

A son was born to her. She named him Perseus. Hearing a baby cry behind the brass door, Acrisius grew furious.

'Who is your husband?'

'The God Zeus, Father. Dare to touch your grandchild, and Zeus will strike you dead!'

'Then I will put you both out of his reach.'

Acrisius locked Danaë and Perseus in a wooden chest, with a basket of food and a bottle of wine, and threw the chest into the sea. 'If they drown, it will be Poseidon's fault, not mine,' he told his courtiers.

Zeus ordered Poseidon to take particular care of the

chest. Poseidon kept the sea calm, and presently a fisherman from the island of Seriphos saw the chest floating on the water. He caught it with his net and towed it ashore. When he knocked off the lid, out stepped Danaë, unhurt, carrying Perseus in her arms.

The friendly fisherman took them to Polydectes, King of Seriphos, who at once offered to marry Danaë. 'That cannot be,' she said. 'I am already married to Zeus.'

'I daresay, but if Zeus may have two wives, why not have two husbands yourself?'

'Gods do as they please. Mortals may marry only one wife or husband at a time.'

Polydectes constantly tried to make Danaë change her mind. She always shook her head, saying: 'If I married you, Zeus would kill us both!'

When Perseus was fifteen years old, Polydectes called him and said: 'Since your mother will not be my Queen, I shall marry a princess on the Greek mainland. I am asking each of my subjects to give me a horse, because her father needs fifty of them as a marriage fee. Will you oblige?'

Perseus answered: 'I have no horse, Your Majesty, nor any money to buy one. However, if you promise to marry that princess and stop pestering my mother, I will give you whatever you want—anything in the world—even Medusa's head.'

'Medusa's head will do very well,' said Polydectes.

This Medusa had been a beautiful woman whom Athene had once caught kissing Poseidon in her temple. Athene was so angered by his bad manners that she changed Medusa into a gorgon—a winged monster with glaring eyes, huge teeth, and snakes for hair. Whoever looked at her would turn to stone.

Athene helped Perseus by handing him a polished shield

to use as a mirror when he cut off Medusa's head, so as not to be turned into stone; and Hermes gave him a sharp sickle. But Perseus still needed the God Hades's helmet of invisibility, also a magic bag in which to put the head, and a pair of winged sandals. All these useful things were guarded by the Naiads of the River Styx.

Perseus went to ask the Three Grey Sisters for the Naiads' secret address. It was difficult enough to find the Three Grey Sisters, who lived near the Garden of the Hesperides, and had only a single eye and a single tooth between them. When Perseus eventually reached their house, he crept up behind them as they passed the eye and the tooth from one to the other. Then he snatched both these treasures and refused to return them until the Grey Sisters gave him the Naiads' address. He found them in a pool under a rock near the entrance of Tartarus, and threatened to tell all the world about them, unless they lent him the helmet, the sandals, and the bag. The Naiads hated anyone to know that, though otherwise good-looking, they had dogs' faces; so they did as Perseus asked.

Perseus, now wearing the helmet and the sandals, flew unseen to Libya. Coming upon Medusa asleep, he looked at her reflection in the polished shield and cut off her head with his sickle. The only unfortunate accident was that Medusa's blood trickling from the bag, in which the head lay, turned into poisonous snakes as it hit the earth. This made the land of Libya unsafe for ever afterwards. When Perseus stopped to thank the Three Grey Sisters, the Titan Atlas called out: 'Tell your father Zeus that unless he frees me pretty soon, I shall let the Heavens fall—which will be the end of the world.'

Perseus showed Medusa's head to Atlas, who at once turned to stone, and became the great Mount Atlas.

As he flew on to Palestine, Perseus saw a beautiful princess named Andromeda chained to a rock at Joppa, and a sea-serpent, sent by the God Poseidon, swimming towards her with wide-open jaws. Andromeda's parents, Cepheus and Cassiopeia, the King and Queen of the Philistines, were ordered by an oracle to chain her there as food for the monster. It seems that Cassiopeia had told the Philistines: 'I am more beautiful than all the Nereids in the sea'—a boast which angered their proud father, the God Poseidon. Perseus dived at the sea-serpent from above and cut off its head. Afterwards he unchained Andromeda, took her home, and asked permission to marry her. King Cepheus answered: 'Impudence! She is already promised to the King of Tyre.'

'Then why did the King of Tyre not save her?'

'Because he was afraid to offend Poseidon.'

'Well, I feared no one. I killed the monster. Andromeda is mine.'

As Perseus spoke, the King of Tyre arrived at the head of his army, shouting: 'Away, stranger, or we shall cut you into little pieces!'

Perseus told Andromeda: 'Please shut your eyes tight, Princess!'

Andromeda obeyed. He pulled Medusa's head from his bag and turned everyone but Andromeda to stone.

When Perseus' flew back to Seriphos, carrying Andromeda in his arms, he found that Polydectes had cheated him after all. Instead of marrying the princess on the mainland, he was still pestering Danaë. Perseus turned him and his whole family to stone, and made the friendly fisherman king of the island. Then he gave Medusa's head to Athene, and asked Hermes would he kindly return the borrowed helmet, bag, and sandals to the Naiads of the Styx? In this way he showed far greater sense than Bellerophon, who had gone on using the winged horse Pegasus after killing the Chimaera. The gods decided that Perseus deserved a long, happy life. They let him marry Andromeda, become King of Tiryns, and build the famous city of Mycenae near by.

As for King Acrisius, Perseus met him one afternoon at an athletic competition. 'Good day, Grandfather! My mother Danaë asks me to forgive you. If I disobey her, the Furies will whip me, so you are safe from my vengeance.'

Acrisius thanked him, but when Perseus took part in the quoit-throwing competition, a sudden wind caught the quoit he had thrown and sent it crashing through Acrisius's skull. Later, Perseus and Andromeda were turned into constellations, and so were Andromeda's parents, Cepheus and Cassiopeia.

THE HUNT OF THE CALYDONIAN BOAR

CHAPTER TWENTY-FOUR

*

THE HUNT OF THE CALYDONIAN BOAR

At the age of only seven days Meleager, Prince of Calydon, caught a fever. The Three Fates happened to stop at the palace on their way back from fighting the Giants. Atropos said: 'His life will last only as long as that log of holly-wood burning on the hearth.'

Meleager's mother pulled the log out of the fire, poured water over the burning end, and hid it in a chest. He recovered, and became the best spearman in Greece.

One day Meleager's father, the King of Calydon, forgot the Goddess Artemis as he sacrificed to the Olympians. When Artemis punished him by sending a huge wild boar to kill his farmers and trample his cornfields, he sent out heralds, inviting heroes from all over Greece to come and hunt it. Whoever killed the boar would be allowed to keep the skin. Most of the heroes had been Argonauts—such as Jason, and Amphiaraus of Argos (who was afterwards killed at Thebes) and the Heavenly Twins, and their rivals Idas and Lynceus, and Ancaeus the *Argo's* steersman, and Meleager himself.

Among the other hunters were Heracles's twin brother Iphicles; and Theseus, famous for killing the Minotaur; and Peleus, husband of the Sea-goddess Thetis; and Meleager's two uncles; and a tall, slim girl named Atalanta; also two Centaurs.

Atalanta's father, the King of Arcadia, wanted an heir to the throne and had been so disappointed when she was born that he ordered his servant to take her up a mountain and leave her there to die. However, Artemis sent a she-bear to nurse Atalanta, who later became a famous huntress and the fastest runner in the world. As an adopted child of Artemis, she swore never to marry.

When Atalanta arrived at Calydon, Ancaeus cried: 'I refuse to hunt with a woman! Women always lose their heads as soon as a boar attacks. They shoot themselves, or their friends, by mistake. Send Atalanta away!'

Meleager answered: 'Certainly not! I am in charge of this hunt. If you dislike Atalanta, go away yourself. She knows more about hunting than you will ever learn. Come, let us all drink wine together and be good friends.'

Ancaeus grumbled, but agreed to stay. He badly wanted to kill the boar.

The wine made the two Centaurs very drunk. They began throwing furniture around, and one of them betted the other that, when the hunt started, he would be the first to steal a kiss from Atalanta.

The horns blew, and the huntsmen went forward through the trees. As soon as the Centaurs tried to kiss Atalanta, she shot them both dead, and walked calmly on. Lynceus saw the boar hiding in an old watercourse, and raised the alarm. It rushed out and killed three hunters. A fourth, young Nestor, who afterwards fought at Troy, yelled and climbed a tree. Jason and the Heavenly Twins threw javelins at the boar. All missed. Iphicles just managed to graze its shoulder. Peleus ran to help a hunter who had tripped over a root, but would have been killed himself if Atalanta had not sent an arrow through its head behind the ear, and sent it off squealing.

'Just like a woman!' shouted Ancaeus. 'Suppose she had missed her aim? That arrow might have hit me. Now watch how *I* fight!'

He swung his battle-axe at the boar as it charged, but only cut the air. The boar's tusks ripped him to pieces. Peleus threw his javelin wildly. It glanced off a tree and killed another hunter—the seventh to die on that fatal morning. At last Amphiaraus blinded the beast with an arrow through the right eye. It went for Theseus, and would have made short work of him had Meleager not run forward on its blind side. He drove his spear under the boar's shoulder-blade deep into the heart.

The monster fell dead. Meleager at once flayed it and gave Atalanta the skin.

'You deserve this, my lady,' he said. 'Your arrow would soon have caused its death.'

Meleager's uncles protested: 'No, Meleager, keep the skin for yourself! You won it fairly.'

'Atalanta drew first blood.'

'That is untrue! Iphicles wounded the beast long before she did. If you refuse to take the skin, let Iphicles have it.'

'Be silent, both of you! I have awarded the boar-skin to Atalanta.'

'You are in love with the girl,' sneered the younger of the uncles. 'What will your wife say?'

'Apologize for that remark, or I shall kill you!' shouted Meleager.

'Why should he apologize?' asked the elder uncle. 'Anyone can see that he has spoken the truth.'

In a rage, Meleager seized his spear and thrust them both through.

Meleager's mother heard that he had killed her two favourite brothers. She took the holly-log from the chest and flung it on the fire.

Meleager felt a sudden terrible burning pain inside him, and slowly died.

Atalanta's father, the King of Arcadia, hearing that she had won the boar's skin, sent a message: 'I am proud of you, my girl. Come and visit me.'

When she arrived at his palace, he said: 'Welcome home! Let me find a husband worthy of you.'

'But, Father, I have sworn never to marry! I hate men!'

'Queen Aphrodite will punish you severely for such talk. Anyhow, as your father I command you to marry whoever I may choose as my heir.'

'Let him catch me first.'

'What do you mean?'

I mean that he must first beat me in a hundred-yard foot-race. I also mean that I intend to kill anyone who fails to win the race.'

The King agreed, grumbling. In the course of the next year or two, Atalanta killed several swift-footed princes. At last a prince named Melanion sacrificed to Aphrodite, and prayed: 'Help me, Goddess!'

Aphrodite lent Melanion the three golden apples which Heracles had fetched from the Garden of the Hesperides, and which Eurystheus had afterwards given her as a present. She told Melanion to throw them on the ground, one after another, during the race. He did so. Atalanta slowed down to pick them up, and lost.

Melanion married her.

THE BEEF-EATING CONTEST

CHAPTER TWENTY-FIVE

*

THE BEEF-EATING CONTEST

Zeus, disguised as a swan, married Queen Leda of Sparta. In course of time, Leda laid a blue egg with three babies inside, one of whom grew up to be Helen of Troy. The other two were the so-called Heavenly Twins. Castor, the elder, became famous as a horse tamer; Polydeuces, the younger, as a boxer. Between them, they won most of the competitions at the Olympic Games, and always kept together.

Their cousins, Idas and Lynceus, twin sons of Poseidon, always kept together too. Idas was a wonderful shot with the javelin, and Lynceus the sharpest-eyed man in the world. He could see in the dark, or find buried treasure by peering closely at the earth. Lynceus first caught sight of the Calydonian boar and raised the alarm; and on the Argonauts' voyage Jason had chosen him to be the *Argo*'s look-out man.

The two pairs of twins kept on good terms during that voyage, and at the Calydonian boar-hunt, because of the common danger; but later Castor and Polydeuces stole the twin sisters to whom Idas and Lynceus were engaged, carried them off, and married them. This would have led to a battle if Idas had not luckily fallen in love with a girl called Marpessa and been glad to let Castor keep his old sweetheart. When the God Apollo tried to take Marpessa from Idas, he cried: 'I love Marpessa more than life itself, Apollo.

Come and fight a duel with me. You have no right to steal men's sweethearts, just because you are a god.'

Zeus admired Idas's courage. He said: 'Marpessa may choose between Apollo and him.'

Marpessa chose Idas, explaining: 'It would be foolish to marry a god. A god always, I notice, deserts his mortal wife as soon as she gets middle-aged. But Idas will be my husband for life. I choose Idas.'

Lynceus also found a wife, and told the Heavenly Twins: 'Now let us all be friends again!'

'Why not?' said Castor. 'What about going to Arcadia, the four of us together, and stealing some of King Iasus's cattle?'

'That should be good sport,' Idas agreed.

Next day, the two pairs of twins stole a hundred and one cows from King Iasus, and beat off the soldiers who came in pursuit.

On their way home, they stopped beside a stream. Polydeuces asked: 'How shall we divide these fairly among the four of us? Four does not go exactly into one hundred and one.'

They drew lots, and Idas was chosen to solve the problem. He killed a cow, sliced it down the middle, roasted both halves, and then said: 'I propose an eating match. This half cow is for Lynceus and myself; that half cow is for you two. Watch: I now cut each half into quarters. Of the hundred cows left, fifty shall go to the man who first eats his quarter share, and the other fifty to the next quickest. Are you ready? Eat!'

Since Castor and Polydeuces had not yet sharpened their knives for cutting off slices of beef, Idas had a short start. And he bolted the meat so greedily that he finished his own share before any of the other three had eaten more than a few pounds. Then he helped Lynceus to eat his share, too.

'We have won all the cows between us,' he announced, wiping his mouth with the back of his hand. 'Come, Lynceus!'

Castor and Polydeuces went on eating. When each had finished his share, they visited Messene, and complained to the city judges. 'Idas started eating too soon!'

'Yes, and Lynceus ate only half his own share.'

'Neither really won a prize.'

The judges answered: 'Wait until Idas and Lynceus come back, and we will decide the case. They are on that mountain-top over there, sacrificing to Poseidon.'

Castor and Polydeuces went angrily off. They hid in a hollow oak tree at the foot of the mountain, intending to murder Idas and Lynceus.

Lynceus had such sharp sight that even while standing beside the altar on the mountain, he could see the Heavenly Twins through the trunk of the tree. 'Aim at that hollow oak,' he whispered to Idas.

Idas took a long run and hurled his javelin. It struck the oak and killed Castor behind. Polydeuces rushed out to avenge his twin. Idas threw part of the altar at him. Polydeuces, though badly hurt, managed to reach Lynceus with his spear.

As Idas bent over Lynceus to see whether the wound were fatal, Polydeuces crept painfully up and stabbed them both to death.

Polydeuces prayed to Zeus: 'Father, let me not be parted from my beloved twin!'

It was fated that one of the Heavenly Twins should be immortal, and the other mortal. Zeus, however, made a bargain with Hades, who allowed them both to become demigods: that is, they would spend half the year in Tartarus, and half on earth.

Poseidon then asked that the same honour should be given his pair of twins.

'No,' said Zeus proudly, 'for my son Polydeuces won the battle!'

THE SEVEN AGAINST THEBES

CHAPTER TWENTY-SIX

THE SEVEN AGAINST THEBES

One day Adrastus, King of Argos, quarrelled with his brother-in-law, Amphiaraus. Adrastus wished to let Polyneices, the ex-King of Thebes, take refuge in Argos. Amphiaraus said: 'No, send him away. He lost his throne because of bad behaviour, and will bring only bad luck on our city.'

Adrastus answered: 'If I decide to give him a home in my palace, what business is it of yours?'

'It is my business to warn you against bad luck.'

'Another word, and I will kill you!'

Both drew their swords. But Eriphyle, who was Adrastus's sister and Amphiaraus's wife, rushed into the room and sent their swords flying with her distaff. 'Now make friends! And promise always to take my advice whenever another quarrel starts.'

They solemnly promised, since she had stopped them killing each other.

Polyneices soon begged Adrastus to help him win back the throne from his brother, who had been made the new King of Thebes. Adrastus promised to declare war on the Thebans, if necessary. But Amphiaraus said: 'I have been warned in a vision that this war will cause many deaths, including my own.'

'Nonsense!' cried Adrastus.

'I beg you to leave Thebes in peace!'

'What business is it of yours?'

Polyneices, knowing that Eriphyle would be called in to settle the quarrel, offered her a magical necklace which he had brought from Thebes—given as a wedding present to his ancestress, Cadmus's wife, by the Goddess Aphrodite. The face of whoever wore it always stayed young and beautiful.

Eriphyle, whose face was growing rather ugly, accepted the necklace eagerly. She then told Amphiaraus that he must obey King Adrastus, come what might.

When the army from Argos reached Thebes, the prophet Teiresias, who was living in the city, warned the Thebans that it must fall unless one of the Sown Men—descendants of those born from the dragon's teeth sown by Cadmus—freely sacrificed himself to the God Ares. A Sown Man at once leaped head foremost from the walls and cracked his skull on the rocks below.

King Adrastus's army was formed into seven companies to attack all the seven gates of Thebes at the same time. Four company leaders fell dead; but so many Thebans also fell that a truce was called and Polyneices offered to fight his brother, King Eteocles, in a duel for the throne. They fought, and each killed the other. At this, the Thebans charged and drove off Adrastus's army. Amphiaraus died when his chariot fell into a ravine; so, of the seven leaders who had started the battle, Adrastus alone escaped.

Many years later, the dead leaders' sons longed for revenge—all except Amphiaraus's elder son Alcmaeon, who advised them against a second attack on Thebes—and Polyneices's son bribed Eriphyle to settle the dispute in favour of war. He gave her Aphrodite's magic robe, another wedding present to his ancestress, which made the body of whoever wore it very graceful indeed. Eriphyle's body by now was growing shapeless in spite of her beautiful face.

The men of Argos again attacked the gates of Thebes, and again were beaten off. This time only one of the seven leaders died—namely King Adrastus's son, heir to the throne of Argos. Teiresias then told the Thebans: 'All is lost. It has been fated that Thebes will never fall so long as Adrastus lives; but he is bound to die from grief when he hears of his son's death. We had better escape from Thebes at once to avoid being massacred.'

The Thebans shouted: 'Oh, Teiresias! Are you perhaps making this up, for fear you will die in the battle?'

'No: I am anxious about your safety, not mine. My life is destined to end tomorrow, whatever you decide.'

That night, everyone stole silently out of Thebes, leaving the army of Argos to break in and plunder the houses when dawn came. Teiresias died the next day, just as he had foretold—bitten by a poisonous snake while he drank from a wayside spring.

The men of Argos returned in triumph with gold and silver, food and wine. Polyneices's son boasted drunkenly of his cleverness in offering Eriphyle the magic robe. So Alcmaeon heard what he had not heard before: his mother was twice bribed to declare war on Thebes, and on the first occasion knew that his father, Amphiaraus, would die in the fighting.

He avenged Amphiaraus by killing Eriphyle. But as he struck the blow, Eriphyle screamed: 'Furies, Furies! Pursue this wretch, who murders his own mother! Of all the lands which the Sun now looks upon, let none give him shelter from your anger!'

The Furies pursued Alcmaeon with their whips. Eriphyle's curse fell on every country he visited. Crops failed, sheep and cows died; he was always ordered to move on. At last he found a piece of land not looked upon by the Sun at the time when Eriphyle cursed him. A great storm had since carried away earth and stones from the mountains of Northern Greece, and formed a new island at the mouth of the Achelous river. There Alcmaeon settled and lived in peace, after marrying the River-god's daughter. The magical necklace and robe were sent to Delphi, where the God Apollo took charge of them, to prevent further mischief.

THE END OF THE OLYMPIANS

CHAPTER TWENTY-SEVEN

*

THE END OF THE OLYMPIANS

When Narcissus was born, his mother consulted the prophet
Teiresias. 'This boy,' said Teiresias, 'will live to a ripe old
age, if he never sees himself.'

Narcissus grew up very handsome, and every woman fell
in love with him. But he sent them all away, saying that he
was not interested in love.

Now, Zeus, when he married Leda, disguised as a swan,
had told a Mountain-nymph called Echo: 'Keep Hera from
following me, please!'

'How?'

'Talk to her. Say anything you like. Invent lies.'

So Echo pretended that she had seen Zeus go off disguised as a woodpecker. Hera listened carefully until she
heard the noise of a woodpecker tapping on a tree trunk,
and then rushed to catch it. But it was an ordinary bird,
and so was the next one she caught.

Hera guessed that Echo had been making a fool of her.
'All right, my girl,' she muttered. 'Your punishment will be
to stay invisible forever, and only able to repeat other
people's words.'

Echo then fell in love with Narcissus; which was awkward, because he could not see her, nor could she start a
conversation.

Narcissus went out hunting one day, and found himself

far away from his companions. Echo followed him. He heard footsteps close by, but saw nobody.

'Is anyone here?' Narcissus shouted.

'Here,' answered Echo.

'Then come to me!' He mistook her for one of his friends.

'Come to me!' she answered.

'Here I am!'

'Here I am!'

Echo rushed to Narcissus and threw her arms around his neck.

He shouted: 'You are a woman. I hate women who kiss me!'

'Kiss me!' Echo begged him.

Narcissus broke away, and ran home.

The Goddess Aphrodite punished Narcissus for being so obstinate. She let him see his own reflection in a pool, as he lay down on the verge to drink, and fall violently in love with it.

Whenever he tried to kiss himself, he only got his face wet and spoilt the reflexion. Yet he could not bear to leave the pool. At last, in grief and disappointment, he killed himself.

'Alas, alas!' he groaned.

'Alas, alas!' groaned Echo, who stood watching near.

'Farewell, beautiful face I love!'

'Farewell, beautiful face I love!' Echo repeated. Then Apollo turned him into the narcissus flower.

As soon as the Emperor Julian of Constantinople, the last of the Roman emperors to worship the Olympians, had been killed fighting the Persians in A.D. 363, Zeus was told by the Three Fates that his reign had ended—he and his friends must leave Olympus.

Zeus angrily destroyed the palace with a thunderbolt, and they all went off to live among humble country people, hoping for better times. But Christian missionaries chased them out with the sign of the Cross, and turned their temples into churches, which they divided among the leading saints. Mortals were now allowed to reckon by weeks again, as Prometheus the Titan had once taught them. The Olympians were forced to hide in woods and caves, and have not been seen for centuries.

However, Echo remains; and so does the narcissus flower, which hangs its head sadly, looking at its reflection in mountain pools; and Iris's rainbow. Moreover, the stars were never given new names by the Christians. You can still see in the night sky the Scorpion that bit Heracles; and Heracles himself; and the Nemean Lion he killed; and Artemis's She-Bear that nursed Atalanta; and Zeus's Eagle; and Perseus and Andromeda; and Cepheus and Cassiopeia, Andromeda's parents; and Ariadne's Crown; and the Heavenly Twins; and Cheiron the Centaur, now known as 'The Archer'; and Phrixus's Ram; and the Bull that carried off Europa; and the winged horse Pegasus; and Leda's Swan; and Orpheus's Lyre; and the stern of the *Argo;* and Orion the Hunter, with his belt and sword; and many other memorials of the Olympians' ancient and savage reign.

INDEX